IMAGES ACROSS THE AGES

RUSSIAN PORTRAITS

Dorothy
and
Thomas Hoobler

Illustrations by
John Edens

RSVP

RAINTREE STECK-VAUGHN
PUBLISHERS
The Steck-Vaughn Company

Austin, Texas

Copyright © 1994 Steck-Vaughn Company

Cover and interior design: Suzanne Beck
Electronic Production: Scott Melcer
Project Manager: Joyce Spicer

Library of Congress Cataloging-in-Publication Data
Hoobler, Dorothy.
    Russian portraits / by Dorothy and Thomas Hoobler : illustrated by John Edens.
        p.   cm. — (Images across the ages)
    Includes bibliographical references and index.
    ISBN 0-8114-6380-X
    1. Russia — Biography — Juvenile literature. [1. Russia — Biography.] I. Hoobler, Thomas. II. Edens, John, ill. III. Title.
    IV. Series: Hoobler, Dorothy. Images across the ages
    CT1207.H66   1994
    920.047—dc20   93-38361
    [B]   CIP AC

Printed and bound in the United States by Lake Book, Melrose Park, IL
1 2 3 4 5 6 7 8 9 0 LB 98 97 96 95 94 93

CONTENTS

"WE CANNOT FORGET THAT BEAUTY"

"Let us seek a prince who may rule over us, and judge us according to the Law." With these words, people of ancient Russia agreed to end their quarrels. They wanted a strong ruler, and sent messengers to the Rus, who lived in the far north. The messengers said, "Our whole land is great and rich, but there is no order in it. Come to rule and reign over us."

Around the year 862, the Rus sent Rurik, a strong and powerful warrior. Rurik and his companions established their control from the town of Novgorod south to Kiev. They made Kiev, "the mother of Russian cities," their capital. Boats traveled north and south along the rivers, bringing trade goods all the way from Constantinople, the capital of the mighty Byzantine Empire.

In the year 980, Vladimir became the Grand Prince of Kiev. He had been raised by his grandmother Olga, a convert to Christianity, but he still worshiped the pagan gods of his ancestors. Then, the ancient Russian chroniclers tell us, "The spirit of the Highest came upon him and enlightened his mind and heart so that he perceived the vanity and error of paganism." Vladimir invited missionaries from all religions to come to Kiev.

Khazarstan, a neighboring state, sent rabbis to explain Judaism, which the Khazar ruiers had adopted. From the east, the country of the Volga Bulgars, came a representative of Islam. A Roman Catholic arrived from Germany and a Greek Orthodox Christian from the Byzantine Empire.

Vladimir listened carefully to the missionaries' views. The Byzantine Christian missionary made the deepest impression on him, but Vladimir wanted to learn more. He sent ten representatives to foreign lands to examine their religious practices. After hearing their reports, he would make his decision.

The ambassadors who had been sent to Constantinople returned, awed by what they had seen:

The Greeks led us to the buildings where they worship their God, and we knew not whether we were in heaven or on earth. For on earth there is no such splendor or such beauty, and we are at a loss to describe it. We know only that God dwells there among men, and their service is fairer than the ceremonies of other nations. For we cannot forget that beauty.

Vladimir made his choice, adopting the Greek form of Christianity in the year 988. To demonstrate his new devotion, Vladimir threw an image of Perun, the Slavic god of thunder with a silver head and gold mustache, into the Dnieper River. The people of Kiev were brought to the riverbank and baptized. Vladimir imposed Christianity on the other cities of his realm as well.

Vladimir's conversion to Greek Christianity was the most important event of early Russia. It gave a unifying sense of purpose to the string of cities that made up the early Rus state. With Christianity came other civilizing influences, including both art and writing. The first Russian paintings were the icons, or religious pictures, modeled after those of the churches in Constantinople. Earlier, a Byzantine missionary, St. Cyril, had created a written form of the Slavic languages. This Cyrillic alphabet, called Old Church Slavonic, became the basis of the Russian writing system.

In the centuries to come, Russians took pride in their strong religious devotion. The elaborate ceremonies of Greek Christianity brought grandeur into the lives of the peasants who toiled on the vast grassy steppes in the south and on lonely farms in the frozen north. From the great churches in Moscow to little wooden chapels in villages, priests led their flocks in prayer and song. In every Russian house, icons of Christ and his mother, of angels and patron saints, occupied places of honor. Russians were born and died underneath their icons, praying to them through times of joy and sorrow. Their faith provided solace and hope when invaders swooped down on Russia from east and west.

With a sense of purpose and destiny, the Russians spread across the largest plain in the world. They would conquer the frozen wastes of Siberia and reach southward to acquire warm-water ports on the Black Sea. Today, even after the breakup of the Soviet Union, Russia is the world's largest country, stretching across 11 time zones from eastern Europe to the Pacific Ocean. The story of this mighty people began with Rurik the Rus.

Battle on the Ice— Alexander Nevsky

The great bell of Novgorod tolled urgently in July 1240. Its ringing summoned the *veche*, or council, which was responsible for the city's welfare. The people of Novgorod faced a danger that threatened all of Russia. Fierce Mongol warriors were ravaging the major cities of the south. At this very time, they were sacking Kiev. And now a second threat appeared: the Swedes were attacking from the north. Invaded from both sides, Russia faced the possibility of utter destruction.

The veche asked young Prince Alexander, already famous for his bravery and courage, to defend the city. The Swedes had built a fort near the Neva River, which was Novgorod's link to the Baltic Sea. Novgorod's all-important trade with the Baltic countries was threatened.

Before long, Birger Jarl, the Swedish ruler, sailed up the Neva River with an army. Moving toward Novgorod, Birger sent a message taunting Alexander—"If thou canst resist me, do so; but I am close upon thee, and am already occupying thy lands."

Alexander appealed for volunteers to defend Novgorod and the Russian Church. He went to the cathedral to pray for success. After receiving the blessing of the archbishop, Alexander encouraged his soldiers with these words: "God is not with Might but with Right. Some trust in weapons, some in horses; but we call on the name of the Lord." Fired up, the Russian troops went to meet the Swedes.

On July 15, Alexander swept into the Swedish camp, catching the enemy off guard. His soldiers, armed with battle-axes and swords, hacked their way to Birger Jarl's gorgeous tent. The Swedish leader managed to escape, but only after Alexander slashed his lance across Birger's face, "putting his seal upon the

foe." After a day-long battle, the Swedes retreated under the cover of darkness. To commemorate his victory, Alexander received the title Nevsky, or "of the Neva."

Alexander Nevsky was born around 1220, the son of Yaroslav, a prince of Novgorod. After Vladimir's time, each of the sons of the Kievan princes had been given a city to rule. This practice eventually caused cities like Novgorod to become virtually independent from Kiev. Novgorod controlled a large area of forest land whose furs, beeswax, amber, and timber formed the basis of a profitable trade. The city took great pride in its wealth and independence. Its proud citizens affectionately called their home "Lord Novgorod the Great."

In Novgorod the process of independence had gone a step further. Instead of a hereditary ruler, the veche now made all important decisions. The *boyars*, or nobles, had no more power than the merchants. The veche elected a prince of the city and designated his duties and powers. If the prince displeased the veche, he could be dismissed. In 1236 Alexander was named prince of the city.

Disaster struck Russia in the thirteenth century. Out of the heart of Asia swept the greatest warriors in history—the Mongols led by Genghis Khan. A Russian chronicler lamented: "There appeared amongst us an unknown people; no one seemed to know anything about them, their language, or their faith, who they were or whence they came, nor to what tribe they belonged."

In 1223 the Mongols attacked and destroyed the kingdom of the Polvetsians, south of Russia. Horror stories about Mongol cruelty spread. Three Russian princes, fighting with the Polvetsians, had been captured. The Mongols had imprisoned them under boards on which they placed their dining tables. As the Mongols sat and feasted, they listened to the screams of their captives, who were slowly squeezed to death.

Then the Mongols returned to their homeland as suddenly as they had appeared. But it was only a temporary retreat because their leader, Genghis Khan, had died. Soon one of his grandsons, Batu Khan, took charge of the Mongol conquests in the west, and he returned with a vengeance.

Batu Khan's warriors were known as the Golden Horde—the Russians often called them Tartars. They destroyed the cities of

Vladimir, Suzdal, and Moscow in 1238. As word spread that they were approaching Novgorod, the citizens panicked. Prince Alexander grimly prepared his defenses. The enemy was within 50 miles of the city when a spring thaw made the marshland too soft for the ponies of the Golden Horde. They turned back and Novgorod was saved.

Other Russian cities were not spared. In the winter of 1240, Batu Khan laid siege to Kiev. It was said that "Men could not hear themselves speak for the screeching of cartwheels, the grunting of innumerable camels, the neighing of horses, and the roar of voices from the multitude of men." Despite a heroic defense, the city fell. The great golden gates of Kiev were torn down, the churches destroyed, and thousands of people slaughtered.

It was at this moment that Novgorod faced the threat from Sweden. The citizens of Novgorod felt betrayed by this attack, for it came from another Christian nation. The pope had encouraged the Catholic Swedes to move against the Orthodox Christian "heretics" in Novgorod. Russians would long remember this stab in the back by European Christians at this most desperate time.

Though Alexander Nevsky received a hero's welcome for his victory over the Swedes, he quarreled with the veche and soon left Novgorod. When a new military threat loomed, however, the veche begged him to return. This time the foe was the Teutonic Knights. The Knights were a military order formed by German princes to forcibly convert their non-Catholic neighbors. The Knights had made some conquests along the Baltic Sea, mistreating Russian "heretics" who had settled in the area. They captured the city of Pskov, which was closely allied to Novgorod.

Alexander Nevsky once more took up arms. He attacked Pskov and quickly wrested it from the Knights. Seventy of the Knights were beheaded, and many German prisoners were sent to Novgorod in chains. Now Nevsky carried the fighting into the Knights' own territory. He advanced to Lake Peipus in today's Estonia, where, in April 1242, the opposing forces faced each other over the ice-covered lake. Alexander raised his hands and prayed: "Judge, O Lord, and settle the dispute between us and this over-bearing people, and not unto us but to Thy Name be glory."

With their coats of armor gleaming in the sun, the Germans rushed forward. At first they drove a wedge into the Russian

forces, trying to separate them into two parts. But Alexander Nevsky saw their plan and counterattacked on the German flank. The battle formation of the Teutonic Knights crumbled and then collapsed. As the German soldiers tried to flee, the Russians pursued, slaying many. Suddenly the ice shattered under the weight of the mounted warriors. Corpses floated for seven miles in the ice-filled water. The battle was remembered as "The Blood Bath on the Ice." This was Alexander Nevsky's greatest military victory, the one that has made him a Russian hero for seven centuries.

When Batu Khan heard of Alexander's triumph, he summoned the prince to appear before him. Every fiber of Alexander's being wanted to scorn the Khan's demand. But he had seen the destruction of other Russian cities. He knew of the Mongols' utter ruthlessness toward their enemies. His concern was for the safety of his beloved city Novgorod. Thus, he agreed to visit Batu at his headquarters at Serai on the Volga River.

At Serai, Alexander saw a city consisting entirely of tents—thousands of them. Soon he was bidden to come into Batu's presence. First, however, he was led between two fires and was told to kneel in reverence to the sun. When Alexander refused, the news was reported to Batu.

Alexander's devotion to his own god favorably impressed the Khan, and their meeting was friendly. Batu granted Alexander's request to free some Russian captives. However, the Khan would not permit Alexander to return to Novgorod. Instead, Batu insisted that he pay homage to the Great Khan of the Mongols at his capital at Karakorum.

The arduous trip was nearly 3,000 miles long, over desert and mountains. Tormented by hunger and thirst, some of Alexander's companions died. But when Alexander arrived, the Great Khan bestowed on him the title of Grand Duke of Kiev. The title made him the most important ruler of the cities of Russia. Yet by accepting it, Alexander also recognized the overlordship of the Mongols and gave them the right to collect taxes and tribute from his people.

He did so, of course, so that Novgorod could avoid the horrible fate of other Russian cities. But the people of Novgorod were not always happy with the situation. Their cherished independence had been diminished. The merchants resented the taxes and tribute collected for the Mongols. From time to time, revolts broke out—one of them led by Alexander's own son. But Alexander firmly put down the rebellions.

To save his city, Alexander made several diplomatic trips to Serai. On his return from one such journey in 1263, he became seriously ill. The prince prepared for his death by taking monastic vows, as was the Russian custom. He asked his followers not to grieve for him, because their distress was troubling his soul.

Throughout Russia the people mourned. When news of Alexander's death reached the city of Vladimir, the archbishop told his congregation, "My dear children, the sun has set for Russia!" The proud citizens of Novgorod prayed for the soul of their brave knight who "labored much on behalf of Novgorod and all the Russian lands."

Over the years many legends and miracle tales arose about Alexander Nevsky. Some Russians believed that he could intercede for them in heaven, just as he had with the Khan. People prayed to him and claimed miraculous cures.

In 1380 the Russians won their first victory over the Mongols in the Battle of Kulikovo. It was the beginning of the end of the 200 years of foreign domination that Russians called the "Mongol yoke." As the fighting raged, many Russians murmured prayers to Alexander Nevsky. After their victory he was made a saint of the Russian Orthodox Church. Ever since, he has been revered as the man who saved Russia in its most desperate time.

CHAPTER 2

THE MILLSTONE—YERMAK

In the year 1577, Ivan IV, the ruler of Russia, ordered a military action against the pirates who infested the Volga River. Ivan IV—who richly deserved his nickname "the Terrible"—ordered his soldiers to catch the criminals and "hang 'em high."

The pirate that Ivan most wanted to catch was Vasily Timofeyovich (Vasily, son of Timofey). So great was Vasily's strength that it earned him the nickname "Yermak," or "the millstone." Yermak was the *ataman*, or leader, of a band of cossacks—a word that originally meant "adventurer." The cossacks were independent frontiersmen of many nationalities. Some served princes as mercenary soldiers. Others were farmers who escaped to the far reaches of Russian territory so that they did not have to pay taxes. Still others, like Yermak, made a living by preying on the weak.

Ivan's military patrol boats sailed down the Volga in search of the pirates. They towed rafts on which gallows were set up to execute their prisoners on the spot. Yermak saw that things were getting too risky. Somehow, he eluded capture and led his band to Perm, a settlement on the Kama River on the northeastern Russian frontier. From here Yermak would start a new and more illustrious career that would add to Russia's greatness.

Yermak was a third-generation outlaw. His grandfather had been a carriage driver in the city of Vladimir who specialized in robbing his passengers. Young Yermak started out as a boatman on the Volga. His strong shoulders made it easy for him to pole the raft carrying passengers and cargo. But he found this life boring and unprofitable. Soon he organized his own gang and began to extort money from wealthy merchants along the river. His murders and robberies eventually brought him into conflict with Ivan the Terrible.

Ivan cast his shadow over Russia in the sixteenth century, ruling from the city of Moscow. Moscow had risen to dominate Russia during the years of Mongol rule. Its people led the fight against the hated enemy and received the support of the Russian Orthodox Church. Under Ivan III (grandfather of Ivan the Terrible), Moscow refused to pay tribute to the Khan. By this time, the Golden Horde had been weakened by internal quarreling and had divided into several separate kingdoms. Ivan III took advantage of the situation by conquering other cities that had once been part of the Kievan state. When Novgorod fell to Moscow's soldiers, they destroyed the great bell that symbolized Novgorod's freedom. Ivan III became the first Russian ruler to take the title *czar*, the Russian form of Caesar.

Ivan IV did not immediately benefit from this new glory. His father died when Ivan was a three-year-old child; five years later, his mother also died. This left Ivan in the hands of the boyars who dominated the court. They treated young Ivan shabbily, and his soul burned with the desire for revenge. At last, when he was 17, he was crowned czar. From then on no one in Russia doubted who was in charge.

Ivan saw enemies everywhere. He personally tortured those boyars who insulted him as a child. He usually carried a staff with a sharp pointed end that he used to impale anyone who displeased him. Married at least 11 times, Ivan had no greater regard for his own children. In a fit of rage, he hit one of his sons with a poker and killed him. He struck such terror in people that they were afraid even while he slept. A diplomat claimed, "He generally drank so excessively at dinner as to fall asleep, and while his guests were all struck with terror and sitting in silence, he would awake, rub his eyes, and begin to joke and make merry with them."

Ivan the Terrible established a special police unit called the *oprichnina*, which hunted down disloyal subjects. Clad in black cloaks and riding black horses with a broomstick and a dog's head hanging from the saddle, the *oprichniki* terrorized the people.

To glorify Moscow, Ivan constructed many beautiful buildings. The most famous is the Cathedral of St. Basil, whose onion-shaped domes are still a symbol of Russia. According to legend Ivan ordered the eyes of the architects plucked out so that they could never create anything else as great.

From the Kremlin, the fortress around which Moscow developed, Ivan continually sought to increase the domains under his control. In the south and east, Ivan's soldiers conquered remnants of the empire of the Tartar khans. This extended Russian territory to the Ural Mountains, the boundary between Europe and Asia.

Ivan coveted the rich booty of the lands east of the Urals, with their gold, silver, and rich furs. Much of the frontier area northwest of the Urals was licensed to the Stroganov family, the richest in Russia. In return for their land grants, they were expected to guard the frontier and bring settlers to the region.

The one-time pirate Yermak offered his services to the Stroganovs. They welcomed him, for the Russian settlements needed someone to defend them from raiders sent by Kucham Khan of Sibir. The Khan controlled the largest and most powerful kingdom east of the Urals. With the Stroganovs' backing, Yermak organized a cossack army of 840 men to carry the fight into Sibir (Siberia).

In September 1581, the expedition set out. Yermak was almost as harsh a leader as Ivan. Anyone suspected of disloyalty was drowned in the river. However, thanks to the Stroganovs, the troops were well provisioned with rice flour, biscuits, salt pork, roasted oats, and butter. Most importantly, they carried firearms, weapons which the Tartars did not possess.

Traveling down the rivers and carrying their boats between streams, Yermak's forces reached the foothills of the Urals just as

winter was starting. They took shelter in a cave, where, according to legend, they buried their treasure from pirate days. Emerging in the spring, they followed the streams of melting snow down the mountains. Soon they entered the domain of the Khan.

Tartar scouts spotted them and planned an ambush. They built a barrier of rope and logs across a stream and hid in wait. When Yermak's men reached the barrier, a hail of arrows rained down on them. As the sun set, they managed to escape upstream.

Yermak was not stopped. He devised a plan to fool the Tartars. Making manikins of twigs and fallen branches, he propped them up in the boats, with only a small crew to man the oars. The rest of Yermak's band crept overland to surprise the Tartars from behind. The trick worked. At dawn the boats floated past the Khan's men, drawing their arrows. Then Yermak's forces cut down the enemy with firearms.

Yermak was keenly aware that he had to capture Isker, the Khan's capital, before the onset of winter or his men would perish in the cold. By October the Russians had marched close enough so that they could see the town in the distance. Yermak's cossacks met the Khan's troops at the bottom of a hill where two rivers came together. Once more, the massed Tartar warriors, armed with bows and spears, proved no match for firearms.

Because he needed reinforcements, Yermak decided to send his second-in-command, Ivan Koltso, to Moscow. This was a dangerous mission, for Koltso, like Yermak himself, was under a death sentence. Yermak thought that the gift of Siberia would change the czar's opinion. But with such an unstable person one never knew. Taking a letter from Yermak, along with furs and some Tartar prisoners as tribute, Koltso and his men set off.

At the Kremlin, Koltso prostrated himself before Ivan and announced Yermak's victory. Presenting the prisoners and furs, Koltso told Ivan that Yermak had annexed the Khanate of Sibir in the czar's name. In his letter, Yermak promised "a vast domain to Russia until the end of time."

Ivan was pleased. He issued a pardon for Yermak and all who had fought with him. Church bells rang throughout Moscow, celebrating the czar's triumph. Ivan sent Koltso back to Siberia with reinforcements and a fine suit of armor—Ivan's personal gift to Yermak.

Yermak continued to add territory in Siberia. He made the natives swear loyalty by kissing a bloody sword. Many did, for the alternative was to be executed by being hanged upside down by one foot. By the end of the summer of 1584, Yermak's control extended almost to the Ob River, one of the three mighty rivers that flow from south to north through Siberia.

In early August 1585, Yermak was lured into a trap. A false report reached him that a Tartar caravan was coming from Central Asia. He rushed to capture its booty. Failing to find it, he and his cossacks encamped on an island in a nearby stream. That night the Tartars attacked.

Yermak's band fought to the last man. Yermak himself, wearing the armor that Ivan had sent him, struggled to reach one of the boats. But a storm had loosed the boat from the mooring and it floated out of his reach. The heavy armor of which he was so proud dragged him to the bottom.

Yermak's achievement endured long after his death. From the foothold he established, the Russians moved across the vast Siberian land, reaching the Pacific within 150 years. Russia thus annexed a territory large enough to contain all of the United States and western Europe combined. Rich in resources, it became a source of wealth for the country, and of misery for the Russians who were exiled to its remote outlands in later centuries.

In death, Yermak was transformed from an outlaw into a national hero. The cossacks celebrated him in one of their epic ballads called *bylini*:

> On the Volga, on the Kama—
> The cossacks lived—the free men!
> Had an Ataman—
> Yermak called they him!
> That this Ataman
> Quietly whispered
> To his bold friend—true
> cossacks, brothers all!
> Here's a thought for you—
> When the summer's gone,
> And the winter's come—where, oh where,
>   shall we spend our time?
> Let us go and take Siberia!

CHAPTER 3

THE PRIEST AND THE LADY— AVVAKUM AND FEODOSIA MOROZOVA

In the winter of 1671, a strange procession wended its way through the snow-covered streets of Moscow. With priests of the Russian Orthodox Church leading the way, a horse pulled a sledge on which a woman lay chained. Crowds of people stopped to watch. Some recognized the prisoner as the Boyarina (or Lady) Feodosia Morozova, a rich noblewoman.

"Bless you!" a woman in the crowd cried out. Others jeered. The story of the Boyarina's crime had spread through the city. She was one of the followers of the rebellious priest Avvakum who had refused to adopt the new rituals of the Orthodox Church. For his defiance, Avvakum had been exiled to a distant region in the Arctic. But Czar Alexis had spared Lady Morozova, urging her to return to the fold of the Orthodox believers.

Now, she was being dragged to prison. Would this public humiliation force her to repent? As if in answer, the Boyarina raised her hand, waving the first two fingers at the crowd. People gasped and murmured. Her message was clear: One of the changes in church ritual demanded that believers use three fingers, instead of two, when making the sign of the cross over one's head and breast.

"Two fingers!" Lady Morozova insisted this was the proper form. Indeed, when her sledge passed a place where she thought the czar himself was watching, she thrust her hand upward as far as the chains allowed. "Two fingers!" Avvakum taught that this was the proper way. Like him, she believed that two fingers were important enough to endure suffering and even death for.

Avvakum was born in the year 1620 in a humble household in a village on the Volga River. His name was the Russian version of

the biblical name Habbakuk, which means "strong fighter." His father, although a priest, "was given to strong drink," according to Avvakum's memoirs. "But my mother was given to fasting and prayer and did most constantly instruct me in the fear of God."

As a boy, Avvakum saw a dead ox at a neighbor's farm. The sight filled him with terror, "and that night, rising from my bed, I wept abundantly for my soul...pondering mortality and how I too must surely die."

From then on, Avvakum prayed nightly before the icons that form an important part of the Orthodox religion. To the devout the glowing faces on the icons radiated the very spirit of their religion. Most icons were painted by monks, for it was believed that only holy men could give them the true spirit. Each night before going to sleep, Avvakum said 600 prayers before an icon of Jesus and 100 before one of Mary, touching his forehead to the ground.

After Avvakum married the daughter of a blacksmith, his mother, content that her duty was complete, entered a convent. Avvakum now became a priest. In the Russian Orthodox Church, priests must be married. They are called the "white clergy." The "black clergy," or monks, take a vow of celibacy.

Avvakum was assigned to a parish, but he preached every-where—"in churches and houses and at crossways, by towns and hamlets." His faith was intense. Once, when evil thoughts torment-ed him, he lit candles and placed his hand in the flames. His fervor attracted the attention of church authorities, who called him to Moscow in the 1640s.

Here Avvakum became part of a circle of priests who were seeking church reform. Among them was Nicon, a priest who was as passionate in his beliefs as Avvakum himself. Avvakum agreed with Nicon that the requirements for priests should be upgraded, for he knew that many did not have the moral qualities needed for their exalted role.

However, their friendship broke down when Nicon became patriarch, or head of the Russian Orthodox Church, in 1652. Nicon used his office to make changes that went beyond reform of the clergy. He believed that over the years, Russian liturgy and ritual had deviated from the original forms from Constantinople. Among these corrections were such changes as the number of times the word *Alleluia* was repeated in rituals. The two changes that caused the most controversy were using three fingers to cross oneself and the spelling of the name *Jesus*.

Avvakum was horrified by the reforms, and he was not alone. To many devout Orthodox followers, the "corrections" were not insignificant (as they might seem to modern readers). Crossing oneself was an ingrained habit among the Orthodox. The act brought blessings to those who faithfully practiced it. Many pious believers feared for their salvation if they changed the form. Others resented what they considered foreign influences among the scholars who made the changes.

The dispute opened a rift in the Russian Orthodox Church that endures to this day. The people who refused to accept the changes were called Old Believers. Avvakum became their leader. In answer to the argument that scholars had merely revived the original ways, Avvakum insisted that the Russians had developed the true belief. He declared, "I am untutored in rhetoric, dialectic and philosophy, but the mind of Christ guides me from within." When Avvakum publicly attacked Nicon from the pulpit, he was banished to Siberia.

For ten years he suffered at the hands of a cruel jailer, Pashkov, who often beat him with a knout, or leather whip. Avvakum was kept in a hole with little food, but none of these punishments broke his faith. While being whipped, "I kept saying, 'O Lord Jesus Christ, Son of God! Help me!' And this I kept repeating without

pause, so that it was bitter to [Pashkov] in that I did not say, 'Have mercy!'" Finally, in 1664, Czar Alexis freed Avvakum and allowed him to return to Moscow.

Czar Alexis was a devout person who regretted the disruption that Nicon's reforms had caused. Bringing Avvakum out of exile was one way he hoped to heal the break. But Avvakum's exile had not changed him. He continued his public attacks on the reforms, and his preaching brought him many disciples. Among them the most highly placed was Feodosia Morozova.

The Boyarina Morozova was a member of the highest nobility. Born around 1630 into a boyar family, she had married Gleb Morozov, one of the czar's officials, when she was 17. Her husband died only a few years later, leaving her to manage his estate and care for their young son. Because she was related by marriage to the czarina, Lady Morozova lived in the *terem*, or women's quarters of the court, when she was in Moscow. Morozova drove about the capital in a carriage made of silver and drawn by 12 horses. At least 100 servants, both men and women, walked behind the carriage to guard her.

Yet Morozova was also deeply religious, and after hearing Avvakum speak, she came under the spell of his powerful personality. When her sympathy with the Old Believer became known, the court was disturbed. Two Church leaders attempted to convince her that she was wrong. But no arguments could sway her from her devotion to her "spiritual Father," as she called Avvakum. As a result she lost her husband's estate, and only the intervention of the czarina saved her from more serious punishment.

Lady Morozova tried not to attract attention and now seldom came to the court. She occupied herself with performing such good deeds as Avvakum describes:

> She kept law and order in her household, inquired personally into the needs of her serfs....She often used to sit down and weave the linen which she afterwards made into shirts for the poor. In the evening, disguised in shabby garments, she would walk the streets of Moscow, accompanied by her faithful attendant, distributing these shirts amongst the poor. She also paid secret visits to prisons and almshouses, bringing gifts of money and clothing. Many a man she saved from imprisonment by paying up his mortgage when it had fallen due.

Often, Lady Morozova gave secret support to Old Believers who remained in Moscow, hiding some of them in her home. As time went on, her house came to resemble a monastery. She herself fasted and stayed up much of the night in prayer. Avvakum—again in exile—wrote her letters of encouragement.

While her son was under her care, Morozova attended the regular Orthodox services with the new rituals. But when he came of age, she made a public break and formally embraced the Old Believer faith. Friends warned her that she was endangering herself.

When the czarina died in 1669, Lady Morozova lost her best protector at court. Two years later, she refused to attend the wedding of Czar Alexis to his second wife—because she didn't want to receive the blessing of a reform priest. The czar was deeply insulted.

In addition, Lady Morozova persuaded her sister Eudoxia, the wife of a prince, to live with her and follow the household's strict religious duties. The czar refused to ignore her defiance any longer. One night the women heard the clatter of horses' hooves in the courtyard. Into their chamber strode officials of the czar and the Church. When the two sisters were asked to declare their loyalty to the Church, they crossed themselves with two fingers—the sign that they were Old Believers. They were arrested.

After her ride through the Moscow streets in chains, Lady Morozova and her sister were imprisoned in a monastery on the outskirts of the city. Again and again they were offered their freedom if only they would renounce their faith. Through more than three years of imprisonment, they steadfastly refused.

Tougher measures came next. When Morozova and her sister refused to attend Orthodox services, they were dragged in chains to the church. News of this spread, attracting crowds of people who were curious to see the two noblewomen. Both women were tortured—chained to a rack and placed over a fire. Morozova taunted her torturer by asking, "Is this Christianity?" One day a message arrived that Morozova's son had died; she was told it was "a punishment from God." Yet she remained true to her faith.

Finally, in 1675, the czar threw the defiant sisters into a filthy dungeon, where they were slowly starved to death. In their last prison, even their rosaries were taken from them, so they tied knots in string to number their prayers. Eudoxia died first, and because there was no priest, Morozova said the prayers for the dead over her body. She soon joined her sister in an unmarked grave. Never during all this degradation did either renounce her faith.

Many other Old Believers were martyred as well, but Czar Alexis hesitated to pass a death sentence on their leader, Avvakum. Some of Avvakum's followers went to join him in his Siberian exile. Indeed, Old Believers—willing to endure almost any hardship to be free to practice their faith—were among the earliest Russian settlers in many areas of the Siberian frontier.

Avvakum did not cease his attempts to convince others of his beliefs. His letters continued to pour out to his flock all over Russia. To get the letters out, he converted his guards into believers. Avvakum wrote down his life story—the first autobiography in the Russian language. It contains many tales that illustrate his fiery personality. Once, a group of traveling performers came to his village of exile. Their acts were described as follows:

> ...dancing bears with tambourines and lutes, and I, miserable sinner, full of zeal for Christ, drove them out. I broke the tambourine and lutes and smashed the clowns' masks out in the field. I alone, against a great number. I took from them two great bears; one I struck senseless, and the other I set loose in the fields. Because of this Vasily Petrovich Sheremetov, who was sailing down the Volga to Kazan, to assume the office of governor, summoned me aboard his ship. He upbraided me and ordered me to bless his son Matthew, whose face was shaven. But I did not bless him and reprimanded him from the Scriptures when I looked upon his lewd countenance. In great wrath the nobleman commanded that I should be thrown into the Volga.

Avvakum's story illustrates two religious points. In ancient pagan Russia, bears were regarded as supernatural creatures. By attacking the bears, he was attacking pagan practices and striking a blow for Christ. His attitude toward the clean-shaven face of the governor's son was similar. To Avvakum, shaving was a heretical practice from the West. As part of their religion, the Old Believers let their beards grow long.

After Czar Alexis died, his son Feodor ordered Avvakum to be burned at the stake. In April 1682, the sentence was carried out. Defiant to the end, Avvakum shouted, "Run and jump into the flames. Here is my body, Devil, take and eat it; my soul you cannot take."

C H A P T E R 4

A Window to the West— Peter the Great

Europe had never seen anything like it before. During 1697 and 1698, the so-called "Great Embassy" from Russia was touring the continent. Among the visitors was a giant of a man, over six and a half feet tall, with the name Peter Mikhailov. His long curly hair, large nose, and piercing eyes made him stand out in a crowd. Although dressed like an ordinary sailor, his true identity soon became known. He was none other than the czar of Russia himself.

Peter was a dynamo of activity, curious about everything. He stopped people on the street to ask them questions about their clothes, even lifting the wigs off men's heads to see how they were made. In the small German state of Hanover, he attended a society ball. Dancing with a woman who was laced in a whalebone corset as was the custom of the time, he commented on how hard the ribs of German women were. In Holland, Peter peeked into the windows of homes to see how the Dutch lived.

The purpose of the mission was to acquire skills and inventions to modernize Russia. Peter visited arms factories in Prussia and spent months working in a Dutch shipyard, learning the secrets of shipbuilding. After watching Dutch doctors perform an operation, he became interested in European medicine. Dentistry particularly fascinated him. Throughout the rest of his life, Peter carried dentist's tongs with him, and loved to pull people's teeth. His officials learned never to mention any dental problems to him, for he would immediately get out his trusty tongs.

Throughout Europe people gossiped about Peter's rough manners, his awkward use of knives and forks, and his strange behavior. People would continue to talk about Peter throughout his 30 years as ruler of Russia, where his actions would earn him the name Peter the Great.

The church bells pealed joyously throughout Moscow in 1672 when a son, Peter, was born to Czar Alexis and his second wife, Natalya. Cannons boomed and fireworks lit up the sky. A gingerbread cake weighing 200 pounds was baked to celebrate the birth. The child's parents pampered and adored him, and his life was a rosy one until the death of his father. Peter was only four.

His older half-brother Feodor became ruler. But Feodor was sickly and died six years later. This set off a power struggle between the families of Alexis' two wives. Both Peter and his feeble-minded half-brother Ivan shared the throne. But Sophia, the ambitious daughter of the first wife, acted as regent. Sophia regarded Peter and his mother's family as a threat. One day, guards forced their way into the quarters of the Kremlin where Peter and his mother lived. In front of the young boy's eyes, they killed his mother's brothers and advisers.

This brutal episode had a great effect on Peter. For the rest of his life he suffered from convulsions. The boy developed a taste for brutality and cruel practical jokes that endangered everyone around him. He kicked and punched advisers who displeased him. People muttered, "To be close to the Czar is to be close to death."

For now, however, Peter and his mother went to live in a home on the outskirts of Moscow. He developed into a gigantic young man of enormous physical strength. He could roll up silver plates as if they were parchment and bend horseshoes with his bare hands. Peter often wandered into the "German quarter" of the city, the section where foreign traders lived. Watching and listening, Peter developed a fascination for Western knowledge and skills.

To amuse himself, he began to play soldiers. Instead of using toys, however, Peter formed his own small army, enlisting boyars' sons and some of his mother's many servants. As he grew older, his games grew more elaborate. He ordered cannons and designed uniforms for his "armies." One set had green jackets; the other blue.

Interestingly, Peter did not demand the rank of general. He believed in merit and felt he did not deserve the position. Instead, he started as a drummer boy, and enjoyed banging out the signals that sent his troops this way and that. After he got the cannons, however, he made himself sergeant of the "bombardiers." A fort was built, and then Peter aimed his cannons and destroyed it.

One day, he came upon the wreckage of an English boat. With

the aid of an old Dutchman from the German quarter, he restored the boat and sailed it on the river. At that time, Russia had no navy; Peter determined that one day he would build one.

When Peter assumed power, he was a young man of 24. He proclaimed that his goal was "to break the bonds of the inflexible customs of Muscovy [Moscow] and to lead [Russia] toward a new day which shall be better than this." Russia was indeed a backward country, with few people who were well educated. A law code issued during Peter's father's reign forbade people to look at the new moon, to play chess, or to fail to attend church. Those who disobeyed were punished with blows of the knout. Nine out of ten Russians labored on farms, most of them as *serfs*—people who were regarded as part of the landowners' property, almost like slaves.

Peter decided that Russia had much to learn from the West. On his trip to Europe, he recruited hundreds of talented people, such as engineers, architects, and artists, to help modernize his country. He cut his trip short, though, when he learned that the *streltsy*, the czar's military guard, had revolted.

Although the rebellion had been put down before he returned, Peter insisted on punishing many rebels himself. He inflicted terrible tortures and beatings on them before cutting their heads off in a mass execution in front of the Kremlin. The lesson was clear—Peter would be merciless to anyone who opposed his plans.

Peter replaced the streltsy with two regiments of guards, many of them his trusted boyhood friends. They now wore their green and blue jackets in a real army.

Peter intended to reform Russia from the top down. He believed that if Russia was to equal the achievements of the Europeans, they would have to copy them not only in skills, but in dress and manners also.

The first step was the elimination of beards. Peter noticed that beards were out of style in Europe, and thus they had to go. Russian men of all classes took pride in their long beards, which they combed into silky mats over their chests. Peter himself shaved the beards of his guards. He then demanded that every Russian male, except peasants and churchmen, shave. Anyone entering Moscow with a beard was directed to a barber. Opposition was fierce. Some men shaved but kept their beards so that they could be placed in their coffins. Peter finally allowed those who wore beards to pay a stiff fine for the privilege.

Similarly, he changed the way Russians dressed. The customary outfit for men was a long flowing robe called a *caftan*. Peter demanded that they shorten their robes or adopt western-style suits. Again, fines were levied on those who refused. Displayed on the gates of Moscow were patterns of appropriate clothes, and guards waited with shears to cut robes.

Women too were told to adopt western dress. Upper-class Russian women often were veiled and lived in the terem. Peter abolished the terem and forbade parents to force a daughter to marry a man not of her choice. He held social gatherings where Europeans would discuss the new ideas, and invited women to come. Some were too shy, but Peter insisted, and had his guards carry them in.

Peter also abolished the titles of the old Russian nobility, the boyars. He created a new aristocracy by awarding titles to those who performed a significant service to the state.

Many leaders of the Russian Orthodox Church were horrified by the reforms. It was whispered that Peter was the Antichrist, leading the country to ruin through his changes. Peter took action. When the patriarch died, he did not name a new one. Instead, he replaced the post of patriarch with the Holy Synod, a council whose members were appointed by the government. Thus the Russian

Orthodox Church lost its independence to the state.

Peter was most interested in building a modern army and navy. Despite the country's huge territory, it had no warm-water ports. The seacoasts of Siberia were frozen for much of the year, and thus unsuitable for trading vessels. Along the Baltic Sea, Sweden held much of the land that had formerly been under the control of Novgorod. Peter decided to take it back. When he attacked the Swedes, however, he found that real fighting was more difficult than make-believe. King Charles XII of Sweden was a great military leader, and his forces soundly defeated the Russians in 1700 at Narva in today's Estonia.

Peter learned quickly; he went back to training his troops and two years later he seized control of the Neva River, where Alexander Nevsky had defeated the Swedes almost 500 years before. The climactic battle between Peter's army and Charles's came at Poltava in 1709. The Russians' decisive victory showed the rest of Europe that Peter had succeeded in making his country a great military power.

Even while the war with the Swedes continued, Peter turned to his most ambitious project. He would build a new city that would be a port from which Russia could develop overseas trade and launch a navy. It would give him his "window on the west." In 1703 Peter cut two pieces of sod from an island in the Neva River, 25 miles inland from the Baltic Sea, and declared, "Here shall be a town." He named the city St. Petersburg, after his patron saint. The Russians who came to live there simply called the city Peter.

The location was not ideal, for the land was marshy. Because it was in such a northern latitude, the river was frozen six months a year. Daylight in the winter lasted only from nine to three. Floods frequently filled the streets with water. To make the buildings secure, they had to be constructed on wooden pilings that often collapsed. But Peter insisted—and he wanted the workers to hurry.

Stone was in short supply, so Peter ordered that no houses could be built anywhere else in Russia while his capital was being constructed. Thousands of prisoners were let out of jail or returned from exile in Siberia to help build the city. In the beginning the workers had few tools. Many dug with their bare hands and carried the dirt away in their shirts. The construction workers slept in the open air and drank foul water. So many of these workers died that it was said the city was built on human bones.

But only seven years after Peter turned the first earth, he had his city. He had always hated Moscow because of the painful memories it held for him. In 1712 he made St. Petersburg the capital of Russia and brought the bones of Alexander Nevsky to lie on the site of his victory. Peter ordered all the noble families to move there.

In his new capital, Peter created Russia's first academies and libraries, hiring teachers from the West to staff the schools. He issued Russia's first newspaper in 1703. Architects from Italy, Holland, and France created the beautiful homes and government buildings. Plumbers brought the waters of the Neva through miles of wooden pipes into the gorgeous fountains that adorned the city. Peter had seen the French king's private gardens at Versailles. At St. Petersburg, he ordered public parks where anyone could stroll. He created some of the gardens himself, ordering seeds and root stocks from all over the known world.

Tragically, Peter's only surviving son, Alexei, opposed his reforms. Alexei became involved with plots to overthrow his father. Peter would not allow disloyalty even from his heir. He told Alexei, "Either change your character, and...be my worthy successor, or become a monk. Give me immediately an answer....If you do not do this, I will treat you as a criminal." When Alexei continued his rebellious activities, Peter had him tortured. Peter himself struck some of the blows of the knout on his son's back. After Alexei died in prison, Peter never again spoke of him.

Peter brought many changes to Russia in government, religion, and the economy. But because the changes were imposed from the top, some had tragic consequences. To pay for the reforms, Peter levied taxes on everything—boots, beehives, hats, even parts of houses such as chimneys. The vast majority of people saw few benefits from these burdensome taxes. Moreover, the forced recruitment of soldiers for Peter's army took young men from every peasant village. Finally, serfdom remained as deeply entrenched as ever, and only the small upper class became westernized. This opened a gulf in Russian society that never healed.

Even so, by the sheer force of his mighty will, Peter had forced Russia to become a great power. By the time of his death in 1725, Russia was an important part of the European community. In the years that followed, it would take a new role in world affairs.

CHAPTER 5

"THE STAR OF THE NORTH"— CATHERINE THE GREAT

On New Year's Day, 1744, a courier arrived at the home of the German prince of Anhalt-Zerbst. He carried a message from Empress Elizabeth of Russia, inviting the prince's teenage daughter, Sophia, to visit her court. The prince understood—his daughter was being considered as a bride for the heir to the Russian throne. At first Sophia's parents were reluctant, for Russia was still regarded as a backward place. Marriage to the future czar seemed an unattractive prospect for a German princess. But Sophia surprised her parents by urging them to accept.

Sophia and her mother traveled by coach and sleigh to Moscow, where the empress was in residence. Sophia knew she was only a prospect, and could be sent home if she did not make a good impression. But she won over Empress Elizabeth, who admired Sophia's rosy skin and bright eyes. Elizabeth also noticed that the young German girl, while very intelligent, appeared to be submissive. That suited the empress very much.

Grand Duke Peter, the czar-to-be, seemed enthusiastic as well. Sophia recorded in her memoirs, "The Grand Duke loved me passionately." Though 16-year-old Grand Duke Peter was short and unimpressive, he was her link to power—and Sophia, even as a 14-year-old, had a strong drive for power.

From the start Sophia set out to impress the Russian court. "God is my witness," she wrote, "that the glory of this country is my glory." She began to study Russian and took instruction in the Russian Orthodox faith. After she converted, she received a new name—Catherine. (The name Sophia brought unpleasant memories of Peter the Great's treacherous half-sister.) As Catherine the Great, Sophia would become the most famous female ruler in all Russian history.

The future empress was born in 1729, the daughter of Prince Christian and his wife Joanna. Christian was in fact somewhat poor for a prince, but he was able to give his daughter a good education. Sophia was tutored in French, which remained her main language for the rest of her life. Sophia adored her father, a devout Lutheran, and believed she inherited her love of learning from him.

On February 9, 1744, Sophia bid her father farewell, never to see him again. He advised her not to abandon Lutheranism, to obey the empress and the grand duke, not to play cards for high stakes, and not to meddle in the affairs of state. Despite her devotion to her father, she disregarded nearly all his instructions.

Her engagement to Peter was announced five months after her arrival in Russia. Just before the wedding, unfortunately, Peter contracted smallpox. For days he hovered near death. When he recovered, his face was horribly scarred. Catherine shut her eyes and went ahead with the marriage anyway. In her memoirs, she wrote, "To tell the truth, I believe that the Crown of Russia attracted me more than [Peter]. Hope for a Crown, not of a celestial order, but very much of this earth, sustained my spirit and courage."

The marriage was a disaster. Peter, never completely normal, seems to have gone over the edge after his illness. He spent his time playing with toy soldiers and now showed a clear dislike for his young bride. Catherine responded by losing herself in reading and studying. She devoured all the books she could obtain, reading about the progressive new ideas sweeping through Europe.

However, Catherine had to survive in a court filled with treacherous people competing for power and influence. No one trusted anyone else. Empress Elizabeth herself was so afraid for her security that she ordered her ladies-in-waiting to talk to her and tickle her feet to keep her awake. Elizabeth's great passion was clothing—at her death she had more than 15,000 outfits in her wardrobe. Some were men's outfits, for Elizabeth gave balls where the men dressed as women and the women as men.

Elizabeth became suspicious of Peter and Catherine. She placed spies in their quarters to report on their every move. Catherine was forbidden to write her mother—or anyone else—without Elizabeth's permission. Catherine got around this by placing notes in the trombone of an Italian musician, who at great risk to himself agreed to forward them. In despair, at one point

Catherine tried to stab herself to death. She was saved by the fact that the knife was too blunt and could not cut through her corset. "For eighteen years," Catherine wrote, "I lived a life that would have rendered ten other women mad, and twenty others in my place would have died of a broken heart."

Catherine took pleasure in riding horses, but the courtiers suggested this was the reason she had not become pregnant. A wiser woman at court, guessing the real reason—that Catherine's husband was not interested in her in any way—introduced her to a handsome young nobleman. In time, Catherine gave birth to a son, named Paul. Empress Elizabeth was delighted, but took the infant away from Catherine to oversee his upbringing herself.

Thus began a series of love affairs which has made Catherine notorious. The most important of her early lovers was Gregory Orlov, an officer of the guards, who helped her in the most important crisis of her life. In December 1761, Elizabeth died, and Peter became ruler. By this time he positively hated Catherine, and she feared that he would send her to a convent.

Luckily, others felt that Peter's behavior was so erratic that it was dangerous to allow him to rule. Within six months Gregory Orlov and his three brothers deposed Peter and placed Catherine on the throne. Ten days later, Peter was killed. No one present could "remember" the details. Catherine rewarded the Orlovs with titles and estates.

Catherine had reached her goal of power. But she was aware of the slim claim she had to the Russian throne. She feared that she could be overturned as easily as her husband. She used all her considerable charm to keep in the good graces of the powerful at court—and she rewarded them handsomely for their loyalty.

Catherine had a good sense of public relations. She staged a grand coronation ceremony for herself to glorify Russian power. It was the custom for each czar to have a new crown. Catherine's crown, made by a Swiss jeweler, was studded with over 5,000 diamonds and topped by an enormous ruby that Czar Alexis had bought from the emperor of China. All the czars after her used this crown, one of the most magnificent ever made.

Now that Catherine finally had the power she desired, she set out to win the good opinion of others, indeed of all Europe. She started to correspond with the leading thinkers of the day—the

French *philosophes* who believed that the world should be looked at through the lens of reason rather than religious faith. In 1764 Catherine heard that Denis Diderot, who had spent years compiling an encyclopedia of all knowledge, was almost penniless. She sent him a large sum of money to "buy" his library, and then let him keep it. When she sought the advice of the famous writer Voltaire on how to govern, the flattered Frenchman sang her praises, calling her the "Star of the North."

Influenced by the philosophes, Catherine developed a plan to reform Russian society. Called the *Nakaz*, or "Instruction," it reflected Catherine's high ideals. It advocated a ban on capital punishment and torture, calling on masters to treat their serfs well. Nobles who did not act in a proper manner would be stripped of their titles. Everyone should be allowed complete freedom of religion.

The Nakaz created an uproar. Not surprisingly, the nobility and church leaders opposed many aspects of Catherine's plan. In the end, she had to give way, finally issuing reforms that were greatly watered down.

Catherine invited Diderot to visit her. He and Catherine spent long hours in discussion. Their talks were very animated. Diderot shook her by the shoulders when she did not understand him, and made his points by pounding her on the thigh. With her body black and blue, Catherine ordered a table to be placed between them to protect herself.

From these discussions she gained a further respect for the new ideas. But she claimed that Russia was not ready for liberal policies. As she remarked to Diderot, "You philosophers are fortunate. Your medium is paper, and paper is always patient. I, Empress that I am, have to write on the sensitive skins of human beings."

When Catherine was 44, a revolt broke out—the most serious one Russia had ever faced. Its leader was Emelian Pugachev, who had been exiled to Siberia for deserting from the army. He escaped in 1773, and began to organize the cossacks of the region around the Ural River. He also attracted support from miners and serfs. Pugachev's original band of 80 men grew to around 30,000 rebels. They pillaged the estates and killed landowners, taking revenge for the appalling conditions under which they had worked.

Pugachev posed a direct challenge to Catherine, because he claimed to be her husband Peter (escaped from Catherine's assassins)—and thus the true ruler of Russia. The rebels moved west to the Volga River. In 1774 they shocked the court by taking Kazan, the largest city in the southwest. Soon the rebels were moving on Moscow itself.

At the time, Catherine's military forces were occupied fighting the Turks south of Russia. She hurriedly negotiated a peace treaty with Turkey, and turned the full force of her army against Pugachev's cossacks. They were soon crushed. Pugachev was brought in a cage to the capital and executed.

The Pugachev Rebellion was a great shock to Russia. Catherine realized why so many of the other rulers of Europe feared the ideas of the philosophes. Liberty and equality were truly dangerous ideas. From then on, instead of improving conditions for the serfs, Catherine increased the landowners' control over them. A law passed in 1785 enabled landowners to punish their serfs by almost any means.

Catherine got the nickname "the Great" for her foreign policy. Her diplomacy was in tune with the morals of her day. Rulers felt it was their duty to expand their territory as much as possible. Catherine added more land to Russia than Peter himself had. With Austria and Prussia as allies, Catherine carved up Poland, with Russia receiving the lion's share. In the first of three "partitions of Poland," she put one of her former lovers on the Polish throne.

Catherine also gained much land from the Turks. She appointed her most famous lover, Gregory Potemkin, to command the troops attacking the Turkish Empire. Russia had long wanted a

warm-water port that would be open to trade at all seasons of the year. Potemkin fulfilled this dream by winning control of the Crimea, a peninsula that extended into the warm-water Black Sea. In 1787 the triumphant Potemkin invited the empress and her guests to inspect the new Russian towns he had built there.

Potemkin prepared a scene that he knew would please Catherine. He gathered peasants from all over Russia and dressed them in colorful costumes. They danced and sang as the empress passed by to give her a picture of happy Russian villagers. When the imperial party approached the port of Sebastopol, where a new harbor had been built, they saw rows of clean, shiny new houses. In fact they were just house fronts, like stage sets, thrown up hastily with nothing behind them. The spectacle gave the world the expression "Potemkin village," which means a trumped-up scene.

Catherine did accomplish many good things. Wishing to spread education, she issued advice to parents on how to bring up their children. She set up the first Russian school for girls, who were taught math and science as well as the arts. She placed a woman in charge of the Academy of the Sciences, the only female in such a position anywhere in Europe. Moreover, Catherine sought to beautify St. Petersburg, a city she loved as much as Peter the Great had. She commissioned a statue of Peter on horseback, which stands today as a symbol of the city. It is inscribed, "From Catherine to Peter."

Catherine was a woman of many contradictions. Though she respected the liberal ideas of the philosophes, she did not let them conflict with her drive for power. Though she added more land to Russia than any former ruler, she claimed peace was necessary for Russia's well-being. Through her influence the court of Russia became as refined as any in Europe. From her time on, French replaced Russian as the polite language of the nobility. However, this only widened the gulf between the upper and lower classes.

Catherine wrote her own epitaph, which shows how she liked to see herself as a ruler:

> Enthroned in Russia, she desired nothing but the best for her country and tried to procure for her subjects happiness, liberty and wealth. She forgave easily and hated no one. Tolerant, undemanding, of a gay disposition, she had a republican spirit and a kind heart. She made good friends.

C H A P T E R 6

"AN AWESOME GIFT"— ALEXANDER PUSHKIN

In July 1814, Czar Alexander I returned to Russia in triumph from Paris. Alexander was hailed as a savior for leading the forces that overcame Napoleon Bonaparte's domination of Europe. His mother planned a gala celebration. Guests from all over the empire gathered at the imperial compound outside St. Petersburg. A victory arch had been built for the czar to pass through. On it were written the words: "O you who return from war, This arch is too small for you."

Among those at the festivities were the students of an exclusive school that occupied part of a nearby palace. Chosen from the best Russian families, the schoolboys wore smart blue jackets with high red collars and three-cornered hats topped with plumes. From their seats overlooking the outdoor theater, the boys listened as speakers compared the czar to the greatest heroes of all time.

One of the boys, however, was busy sketching. Alexander Pushkin had an impish sense of humor, and all this pomp and ceremony stimulated his imagination. On his sketch pad, he drew a grossly fat caricature of the czar approaching the victory arch. The arch, it was clear, was too narrow to allow the czar to pass through. Alexander sketched a group of alarmed generals hacking at it with their swords, attempting to make it larger. As the drawing was passed around, Alexander's schoolmates snickered at his witty commentary on the noble words over the arch. Few could have guessed that Alexander Pushkin would become more famous than the conquering czar himself, as Russia's most beloved poet.

Pushkin was born in Moscow on May 28, 1799. His father was from an old noble family. On his mother's side, Alexander was descended from an Ethiopian prince named Ibrahim Hannibal. As a

child, Ibrahim had been captured by Turks who took him to Constantinople as a hostage. Later the Turks sent Ibrahim to Peter the Great as a gift. Peter was so impressed by the boy's keen intelligence that he sent him to Paris for schooling. Ibrahim later became a general in the Russian army, and his granddaughter was Alexander Pushkin's mother. Alexander's dusky complexion reflected the African origin of his great-grandfather. Throughout his life, Alexander was proud of his heritage on both sides of his family.

Alexander's self-centered parents showed little love for their children. His happiest childhood memories were of his nanny, an old peasant woman. She told him the old fairy tales and proverbs that gave him a deep love of Russian customs and life.

At 12, Alexander was accepted at the Lyceum, a school that the czar had established outside St. Petersburg. Here, Alexander was out of harm's way when Napoleon invaded Russia in 1812. The invasion brought all Russians together in the effort to repel the French. It was a time of great patriotism and pride.

Napoleon's troops marched all the way into Moscow. But the Russians burned the city, leaving no food or supplies behind. When the harsh winter set in, Napoleon was forced to retreat. Along the way, Russian troops attacked the French army again and again. Napoleon lost the best part of his once-mighty army in Russia, and never recovered. Two years later, Czar Alexander rode at the head of the Russian troops when they entered Paris.

Meanwhile young Alexander Pushkin was enjoying a happy life at school, where his sense of humor and love of pranks made him many friends. Pushkin enjoyed sneaking out at night and drinking in taverns. Still, his talent was already so great that the school overlooked his unruly nature. The minister of education chose him to write a poem for the wedding of the czar's sister.

Though Pushkin was already well known as a poet when he graduated in 1817, he took a job in the Foreign Office. Immediately he began to enjoy the high and low life of St. Petersburg. Small and lithe, Pushkin was an accomplished swimmer, horseman, and swordsman. He also developed a lifelong passion for gambling. Pushkin was very much like the dashing hero of his epic poem, *Eugene Onegin*:

> His hair cut in the latest mode;
> He dined, he danced, he fenced, he rode.

In French he could converse politely,
As well as write; and how he bowed!
In the mazurka, 'twas allowed
No partner ever was so sprightly,
What more is asked? The world is warm
In praise of so much wit and charm.

Welcomed into the fashionable homes of the capital, Pushkin entranced women both young and old with his dark, penetrating eyes, his skill at dancing the mazurka, and his way with words. However, their husbands or suitors were quick to take offense, and in those days such matters of honor required a duel.

Duels were fought with precise ceremony. The two opponents appeared at an agreed-on spot, accompanied by seconds. After stepping a certain number of paces apart, the two duelists aimed their pistols at each other and fired. With the limited range of the pistols, usually (but not always) no harm was done. The purpose was to satisfy the demands of honor. One of the poet's friends remarked, "Pushkin fights duels every day; thank heavens they are not fatal."

Pushkin published his first long poem, called *Ruslan and Ludmilla*, when he was 21. Based on a Russian folktale, it caused a sensation. No one could recall there being a poet so young with this kind of talent.

Pushkin enjoyed sending his new poems to friends and fellow poets, with whom he shared the hope for greater freedom and reform in his homeland. Czar Alexander had hinted that he would end serfdom and grant his country a constitution, but nothing came of it. Pushkin wrote:

O, but if my voice could only move the heart!
Why else this barren passion in my breast should burn
But for this awesome gift of speech bestowed on me by Fate?
When will I see, O friends! the masses free
And slavery struck down by the Sovereign's own hand,
When will that beautiful dawn of freedom so enlightened
At last arise above our land?

The czar's censors, who were authorized to punish any author who wrote "dangerous" material, read one of his unpublished poems in an intercepted letter. Pushkin feared he would be exiled to Siberia, but his fame and friends saved him. Instead, he was sent to sunny Bessarabia in the southwest.

Here he continued his wild life-style. When he accused a man of cheating at cards, the man challenged him to a duel. This was a common occurrence to Pushkin. He showed up eating cherries. As his opponent raised his pistol, Pushkin nonchalantly spat cherry pits at him. When the other man's shot missed, Pushkin didn't bother to fire back. He wandered away, still eating the cherries.

Rumors of Pushkin's wild antics reached the capital. The government, irritated at his behavior, exiled him to his mother's estate in the north near Pskov. The main house there was filled with the furniture of his African great-grandfather. Happily, Pushkin's old nanny joined him there. He wrote his brother:

> Do you know how I spend my time? Before lunch, I write. I eat late. Afterward, I ride. In the evening I listen to my nanny's tales....What wonders they are, her old tales! Every one is a poem....Sometimes she is cleverer than I am, because...she is closer to the truth.

Solitude gave him time to think about his art. Unlike earlier Russian authors, he did not seek to imitate French styles and examples. Instead, having absorbed European culture, he used to the full all the riches of the Russian language and heritage. At his mother's estate, he began writing one of his great masterpieces, *Eugene Onegin*, which he would work on for seven years.

Pushkin's exile saved him from becoming involved in the Decembrist Revolt of 1825. After the death of Alexander I, some officers and aristocrats plotted to overthrow the new czar, Nicholas I. Their plans were discovered, and the revolt was foiled. Five conspirators were hanged and many others exiled to Siberia. Some of the plotters were friends of Pushkin. When copies of his poems were found in their apartments, the czar's officials were suspicious.

The new czar called Pushkin to St. Petersburg in 1826 for a private talk. No two men could have been more different. Nicholas was a man of iron discipline. Tall and arrogant, he wore his military uniform on all occasions. Pushkin was a free spirit who lived life to the fullest. When the czar asked him about the Decembrists, Pushkin admitted that had he been in St. Petersburg, he might have joined them. Nevertheless, the czar made a startling proposal. He

ordered Pushkin to show him everything he wrote. If the czar approved of it, the work would be published. Pushkin would be free of all other censorship.

Pushkin resumed his merry life in the capital, but the czar's officials kept their eyes on him. He was listed in the police files as "No. 36, Pushkin, well-known gambler." Despite some problems with the czar over censorship, it was a period of great creativity. He published his play about Boris Gudunov, a czar in the early seventeenth century; "The Queen of Spades," a famous short story about a gambler; and a novel about Pugachev's Rebellion.

Pushkin's work made him famous far beyond the drawing rooms of St. Petersburg. Everywhere in Russia, it seemed, people knew about him. Even peasants who could not read heard lines of his poems read aloud, and in his own lifetime he became an almost mythical figure. The possession of artistic skills was regarded as a divine mystery in Russia. The poet was considered to be a sublime being because of his art. Pushkin used the Russian language to express the deepest feelings of the Russian people.

His works have been described as "an encyclopedia of Russian life." From the rich storehouse of his writings, future Russian artists in all fields would draw inspiration. Painters used scenes from his work as their subjects. Musicians took the stories and used them as the basis for operas or ballets.

Pushkin fell deeply in love—with the most beautiful girl in the city, Natalia Goncharova. Sixteen years old, she had a slim figure and dark hair. The poet asked her to marry him. At first, Natalia's mother opposed the match, believing her daughter could marry a wealthier man. But at last she gave her permission, and the wedding took place in 1831. There were bad omens at the ceremony. Nervously the groom dropped a crucifix from his hand, and after a candle was lit to celebrate the union, it went out.

What Pushkin did not realize was how empty-headed his wife was. She had no interest in his work, caring only for the extravagant balls that were part of the St. Petersburg social life. Pushkin had grown tired of these empty social events. His wife's clothing bills—along with his gambling debts—gave him constant worries about money. The marriage deteriorated.

Still Pushkin kept up his astonishing output of work. He began his long poem *The Bronze Horseman*, reflecting his continuing concern with Peter the Great and his city. The statue that Catherine dedicated to her predecessor seemed to brood over the capital. The poem tells the story of Evgeny, who loses his beloved when floods engulf the city in 1824. When Evgeny curses the statue, the bronze horseman jumps off his pedestal and pursues him. In the poem, Pushkin displays his love/hate feeling toward the capital, contrasting its greatness with the tremendous human cost of building a city in such an unfavorable spot. It reflects the helplessness of the "little hero," Evgeny, against the power of ambitious rulers. The poem, not published till after his death, is one of his great masterpieces.

When Natalia took up with another man, Pushkin felt humiliated and angry. He challenged his rival to a duel. This time the poet's opponent fired in earnest. Pushkin was carried home, mortally wounded. As word of his death spread through the city in 1837, throngs of people gathered at his house. For three days, Russians of all classes—nobles, students, children, peasants who came from their fields—passed by the coffin of the poet who had given Russia a voice. Another poet expressed the Russians' special feeling about Pushkin and his poetry: "You, like first love, the heart of Russia will not forget."

CHAPTER 7

"WHAT AM I DESTINED FOR?"—
LEO TOLSTOY

"I am 24 years old and I have still done nothing," Leo Tolstoy wrote in his diary. "I am sure it's not for nothing that I have been struggling with all my doubts and passions for the past eight years. But what am I destined for? Only time will tell." The day was his birthday—August 28, 1852.

The majestic mountains of the Caucasus, with their boiling hot-water springs, loomed before him. Young Leo had gone there to join his older brother Nicholas in the Russian army. It was the romantic dream of young Russians to find glory in this wild place, fighting the Muslim tribesmen. That very day, Leo had been under fire for the first time. He took pride in the fact that he did not flinch. "It is so good to be alive," he wrote, "nature is so beautiful."

Yet Leo was unsure what he wanted to do with his life. He tried writing in his spare time, and had sent a story titled "Childhood" to a magazine. Like any young writer, Leo eagerly awaited a response.

The day after his birthday, he received the answer— "Childhood" had been accepted. Leo was thrilled. It was the beginning of a career that would bring him fame and wealth. Tolstoy's great novels are loved the world over. But success did not bring him contentment. Throughout his long life Tolstoy remained a restless soul who never stopped asking the question, "What am I destined for?"

Leo Tolstoy was born on August 28, 1828, in the manor house of Yasnaya Polyana ("Clear Glade"), an estate about 140 miles south of Moscow. The estate belonged to his mother's side of the family, the Volkonskys, who traced their ancestry back to the first rulers of Russia. One of Tolstoy's ancestors had received the title of

"count" from Peter the Great. But Leo's grandfather had frittered away his wealth through extravagant living. He sent his laundry all the way to Holland to be washed, had his fish shipped directly from the Black Sea, and hosted many balls and other expensive entertainment. Nicholas Tolstoy married Marya Volkonsky, and thus gained Yasnaya Polyana. She gave birth to a daughter and four sons, of whom Leo was the youngest. She died when Leo was only 18 months old.

Leo idolized his oldest brother, Nicholas. Together they skated in the winter, collected mushrooms in the summer, and played in the fields around Yasnaya Polyana. Nicholas told Leo about a green stick with a message on it that would bring happiness to all people. Nicholas believed the stick was buried near a ravine in a grove of trees. This was Leo's favorite place. Years later, he wrote in his will that he should be buried in the grove where he had searched for the magic green stick.

At 16 Tolstoy enrolled in the University of Kazan. Hoping to be a diplomat, he studied Arabic and Turkish, but finding languages difficult, he switched to law courses. Doing no better in these, he finally left school.

Still looking for a career, Leo went off to the Caucasus to serve with Nicholas. During the Crimean War of 1854-1856, he took part in the defense of the Russian naval base at Sebastapol. A combined force of British and French troops captured the base after a long siege. The defeat humiliated Russia. Although angered by the corruption and incompetence of the government, Tolstoy had great respect for the courage of the soldiers he commanded, who fought bravely under the most difficult conditions.

He resigned from the army and spent the next six years living in Moscow and St. Petersburg and traveling through Europe. In Britain he met Charles Dickens, whose novels he admired greatly. In later years Tolstoy kept Dickens's portrait on his writing desk.

Tolstoy had seen soldiers die in battle, but in Paris, the sight of a public execution on the guillotine disgusted him. He wrote strongly in opposition to the death penalty. Another death stunned him further. While in the south of France, he visited his brother, who had contracted tuberculosis. Holding Nicholas in his arms, Tolstoy watched him die. Later he wrote that the death of his brother was "the most powerful impression of my life."

Tolstoy returned to Russia in 1861, the year Czar Alexander II freed the serfs. Tolstoy enthusiastically supported the emancipation; he had long considered freeing the serfs who worked on his own estate. Now he paid his former serfs as regular workers, and opened a school at Yasnaya Polyana for them and their children. To show that he believed they were his equals, he dressed in peasant clothing and worked alongside them in the fields.

The following year, at age 34, Leo married a young woman of 18—Sophia Behrs, the daughter of a Moscow doctor. During an often stormy marriage lasting 48 years, she bore him 13 children. In the happy early years of his marriage, Tolstoy started work on his massive novel, *War and Peace*. It would take him almost seven years to complete. During this immense labor, Sophia bore four children and shielded Tolstoy from all the cares of managing the estate. She took over the business accounts and the raising of the children.

Still, Sophia found time each night to copy what Leo had written that day. Almost no one else could make sense of his tiny scrawl, with sections crossed out and corrected between the lines or on the back of the page. Working by flickering candlelight, she wrote out a fresh copy in her clear handwriting and placed it on his desk. The following night Sophia would find her beautifully neat copies covered with more changes. Patiently she transformed them once again. By the time her husband had finished the novel, she had copied the mammoth book seven times.

Often Tolstoy himself did not know in advance what would happen to the characters he created. When he was discouraged, he would lay out a game of solitaire on his desk, saying, "If this game comes out, I'll have to change the beginning," or "The cards will tell what happens next."

Set during the Napoleonic wars, *War and Peace* is one of the world's greatest novels. It follows three fictional families through the tempestuous time of Russia at war. For many characters, Tolstoy used family members and friends as models, mixing them with the "juice of fiction." Real historical characters, such as Napoleon and the Russian general Kutuzov, also appear. Although the novel contains many battle scenes, Tolstoy was most interested in the experiences of people caught up in the huge historical event. Romance, ambition, pain and loss, happiness and triumph—all are part of the grand saga.

Tolstoy understood the human heart so well that his writing has a timeless quality. The book's heroine, Natasha Rostova, while getting ready for her first ball, worries like a teenager of today: "Is it possible no one will ask me, that I shall not be among the first to dance?"

At a later party, Natasha asks one of the older guests to dance:

Denisov...unhooked his saber. He came out from behind the chairs, clasped his partner's hand firmly, threw back his head, and advanced his foot, waiting for the beat....he looked sideways at his partner with a merry and triumphant air, suddenly stamped with one foot, bounded from the floor like a ball, and flew round the room taking his partner with him....Natasha guessed what he meant to do, and abandoning herself to him followed his lead hardly knowing how. First he spun her round, holding her now with his left, now with his right hand, then falling on one knee he twirled her round him, and again jumping up, dashed so impetuously forward that it seemed as if he would rush through the whole suite of rooms without drawing breath, and then he suddenly stopped and performed some new and unexpected steps. When at last, smartly whirling his partner round in front of her chair, he drew up with a click of his spurs and bowed to her, Natasha...fixed her eyes on him in amazement.

After finishing the book, Tolstoy was exhausted. In 1870 he wrote, "All this winter I have done nothing but sleep, play bezique [a card game], ski, skate and run, but mostly lie in bed." He walked among the birches and pines on his estate, enjoying the calm and beauty of nature. It was a time to play with the children and ride and hunt. He also wrote primers for his peasant school. He firmly believed that the material should always be interesting and that the child should never be afraid of the teacher.

Ideas continued to percolate in Tolstoy's restless brain. One evening, he began to read one of Pushkin's stories to Sophia and inspiration struck. He started to write the novel that would become *Anna Karenina*. It tells the story of a woman who leaves her loveless marriage, her family, and high social position to follow her lover. At first, Tolstoy intended the heroine to be an unsympathetic person, but as he wrote, he fell more and more in love with her. For four years he worked on the manuscript. At the end of the novel, Anna commits suicide by throwing herself under a train. Her tragic fate seems to have caused a crisis in Tolstoy's own life.

Two years after completing this second supreme masterpiece, Tolstoy renounced all his past achievements. His military service, he decided, had made him a killer. Even the success of his books seemed an empty triumph; he believed they did nothing to add to the betterment of humankind. From that point on, he followed a personal quest for the meaning of life.

Tolstoy was always a driven man, torn between the pleasures of life—which he enjoyed to the full—and the spiritual goal of personal salvation. He was never able to reconcile these two conflicting halves of his personality. Wealth, fame, talent, praise—all these were impediments to his quest. Yet, try as he might, he could not escape them.

It was typical of his great soul that he wished to save not only himself, but all humankind. He began to write tracts setting forth his religious beliefs and welcomed to his home others who shared his yearning for spiritual values. He spent a great deal of time working in the fields with the peasants and even tried to give away his wealth. His wife Sophia, concerned for the welfare of their children, prevented him. Their marriage became strained, for Sophia had no sympathy for his religious ideals.

Tolstoy had been raised in the Russian Orthodox Church, but

as he grew older, he lost his faith in any organized religion. He regarded rituals and sacraments as unnecessary distractions. He wrote that people should only look inside themselves for truth—"The kingdom of God is within you." Because of his unconventional views, expressed in his later writing, the Russian Orthodox Church excommunicated him in 1901.

Eventually Tolstoy developed his own system of personal ethics. He condemned violence of any kind, declaring that people should protest evil in a nonviolent way. Because he was the greatest Russian of his time, his views attracted attention throughout the world. One person who was deeply influenced by them was Mohandas Gandhi, a young Indian lawyer. Gandhi adopted Tolstoyan beliefs into his own form of nonviolent resistance and would use them to lead India to independence. Martin Luther King, Jr., the United States civil rights leader, was also influenced by Tolstoy's ideas.

In Tolstoy's later years, pilgrims flocked to Yasnaya Polyana as if it were a religious shrine. Visitors were expected to share the work in the fields. People from around the world wrote to the great man, seeking his advice. Thomas Edison sent one of his new inventions—the dictaphone—asking Tolstoy to make a recording of his voice. But Tolstoy became so nervous when he tried to speak into it that he stuttered and forgot what he was going to say. "Stop the machine," he cried, "it's dreadfully exciting." He added, "Probably such a machine is good for well-balanced Americans, but it is not good for us Russians."

As time went on, the relationship between Tolstoy and his wife grew worse. More and more, he felt he could not pursue his real goals while living at his estate. In 1910 Tolstoy put on plain work clothes and fled his home in the middle of the night. He was determined to wander for the rest of his life as a penniless pilgrim.

Accompanied by his youngest daughter, Tolstoy did not get far. In the cold winter, he caught pneumonia and collapsed on a train. He was taken to the house of the stationmaster in the little town of Astapovo, about 120 miles southeast of Moscow. There he died on November 7, 1910. His body was returned to Yasnaya Polyana and buried in the grove of trees where he had sought the magic green stick as a child. At last he had found the peace that had always eluded him.

CHAPTER 8

"OH, THE MUSIC!"— PETER TCHAIKOVSKY

In the winter of 1868, Peter Tchaikovsky was in high spirits. The young composer's first symphony had just been performed before an enthusiastic audience. Thus, when he received an invitation to conduct some dances from his new opera at a public performance, he accepted. It was for a good cause; the proceeds from the performance would go to help famine victims.

Peter was a terribly shy person, always ill at ease in unfamiliar situations. He had never before conducted his own works. Yet he felt fine, not at all nervous, until he reached the stage. When he saw the audience, a terrible fright came over him. Tchaikovsky had a hallucination that his head was about to fall off. As the orchestra began to play, he lost the beat of the music. He pointed his baton at the musicians at the wrong times, urging them to play when they were not supposed to. Worse yet, Tchaikovsky kept reaching up with his other hand and pulling at his beard, so violently that his head jerked back and forth. He later confessed he was trying to keep his head on.

Fortunately the musicians ignored Tchaikovsky's erratic behavior and got through the performance in spite of him. Tchaikovsky was so humiliated that he did not conduct again for ten years.

Peter Tchaikovsky was born May 7, 1840, in Votkinsk, a city in central Russia. His father, Ilya, was a geologist and inspector of mines. Madame Tchaikovsky was of French descent, and the object of her young son's adoration. Peter was a sensitive child, very high-strung but charming. Any scolding would send him into fits of crying and depression.

Peter started playing the piano at the age of five. He loved it so

NADEZHDA VON MECK

much that he would drum his fingers on a window when he was not practicing. One day he became so excited that he broke the glass and cut his hand.

The Tchaikovsky family tutor, named Fanny, thought that music was too disturbing to young Peter. She tried to discourage him from playing the piano. One night, after the children had attended a party where music had been played, Fanny found Peter weeping in his bed. "Oh, the music!" he cried, pointing to his head. "It's there, in there. It won't let me rest."

At the time of Peter's childhood, Mikhail Glinka was Russia's most famous composer. Glinka used Russian folk songs in his operas and compositions. The Russians, then as now, loved music and made it part of their lives. From early times, Russians celebrated the events of the year by singing—rounds and dances, carols at Christmas and Epiphany, fortune-telling songs, and love songs. As a youth Peter heard the peasants singing in the fields to make their labor easier. Music was all around him.

However, the Tchaikovskys wanted their son to have a career in government. When Peter was ten, his mother took him to a boarding school in St. Petersburg. When she left, he was so distressed that he ran after her coach, trying to cling to its wheels. Four years later, her death from cholera left him devastated. Throughout his life Peter remained devoted to her memory.

Later, Peter's father enrolled him in a law school in the capital. He still played the piano to amuse friends, but meekly accepted the career that his father had planned for him. On graduation he obtained a job as a clerk in the justice ministry. For four years Peter moved papers back and forth, so bored that in later years he could never recall anything that he did there.

Tchaikovsky haunted the concert halls of St. Petersburg, attending operas and ballets. He signed up for music classes and entered the newly created Conservatory of Music in 1862. The school's director, Anton Rubinstein, was an inspired teacher and composer. When Rubinstein complained that Peter was not devoted enough to music, he resigned from the justice ministry. For years, even after becoming a famous composer, Peter yearned to hear words of praise from his old teacher. Alas, Rubinstein never had a high opinion of his most famous pupil's work.

After graduation Tchaikovsky went to teach at the new

Conservatory at Moscow, which was headed by Nicholas Rubinstein, Anton's brother. Nicholas saw talent where his brother had not. With his encouragement Tchaikovsky began to write a symphony, called *Winter Daydreams*. He suffered from nightmares and hallucinations while working on it.

Unfortunately the audience at the symphony's first performance in Moscow did not appreciate the music. Tchaikovsky's unhappiness lasted for two years until another audience applauded so loudly that he was called on stage to accept their praise. This success was followed by his disastrous debut as a conductor.

Throughout his life Tchaikovsky was always uncomfortable in social situations. He wrote, "By nature I am a savage. Every new acquaintance, every fresh contact with strangers has been the source of acute mental suffering." Tchaikovsky was a strange blend of madman and genius. Despite his tormented inner life, he was to write some of the world's most beautiful music.

In 1876, Tchaikovsky received a letter from Nadejda von Meck, a wealthy widow who loved music so much that she kept a string quartet at her estate. After hearing Tchaikovsky's music, she offered him money to support his career, on one condition—they must never meet in person.

It was the start of an unusual friendship, but one that suited the intensely shy composer. For 13 years Tchaikovsky wrote letters to Madame von Meck, pouring out his thoughts in a way that he could not have done face to face. In 1878 he finished his Fourth Symphony, dedicating it to Madame von Meck, "My Best Friend." He was in Italy when the symphony had its premiere in Moscow. His spirits soared when Madame von Meck wrote him that the symphony had touched her heart. She spared him the news that the audience and the critics were not so enthusiastic.

Madame von Meck offered not only financial support, but praise and encouragement that Tchaikovsky desperately craved. Thus he was stunned when she suddenly cut off the relationship in 1890. Although Tchaikovsky no longer needed her financial support, he felt abandoned. It was like losing his mother all over again.

In the meantime Tchaikovsky had gained another important patron. In 1880 he wrote a patriotic work to celebrate the silver jubilee of Czar Alexander II. The composer tried to recreate in music the Russian victory over Napoleon in 1812. As the piece begins, the national anthems of France and Russia seem to battle each other. At the climax, as the Russian anthem swells triumphant, the audience is startled by the sounds of cannon and church bells. This was the *1812 Overture*, one of the most popular works of music ever composed. Yet Tchaikovsky seemed embarrassed by it. "The *Overture* will be very loud and noisy," he wrote, "but I wrote it with little warmth or love; therefore it will probably have small artistic worth."

However, the *1812 Overture* greatly pleased the royal family. For the coronation of Alexander III, Tchaikovsky wrote a special march. In appreciation the new czar sent him a diamond. Three years later Alexander decorated Tchaikovsky with the Order of St. Vladimir—Russia's highest honor.

Tchaikovsky was an ardent patriot. "I passionately love Russia, the Russian language, the Russian way of thinking, the Russian facial beauty, Russian customs," he wrote. Like other Russians he felt sympathy for other Slavic people in their fight for independence from the Turks. When the Serbians were at war with Turkey, Peter wrote a new piece, the *Marche Slav*, to commemorate the gallant Serbian fighters.

The czar was pleased; he asked Tchaikovsky to conduct the *Marche Slav* himself. It isn't hard to imagine Peter's feelings. The last time he had mounted the podium was the disaster in 1868. But it was impossible to refuse the czar's request. This time everything went smoothly—no fear, no hallucinations. As the orchestra played the final notes, the Russian ruler stood and applauded, demanding an encore. From then on Tchaikovsky lost all fear of conducting.

Indeed, he began to accept some of the many invitations that his growing fame had brought him. First he did several tours of Europe; then in 1891 he went to the United States, where he conducted the very first concert held at New York's Carnegie Hall.

Again, though, his peculiar nature bedeviled him. Whenever he left Russia, he immediately became homesick. Yet no sooner was he home than he wanted to go away again. Nervousness and vague fears constantly tormented him. "The greater reason I have to be happy the more discontented I become," he wrote. "A worm continually gnaws in secret in my heart." Not even success could quiet his nerves. He always seemed to have a letdown after any triumph.

In his self-imposed periods of solitude, Tchaikovsky read

widely. He loved Pushkin's writings and based several musical pieces on them. His two greatest operas, *The Queen of Hearts* and *Eugene Onegin*, are based on Pushkin's stories.

Tchaikovsky wrote some of his greatest music for the ballet. A Pushkin poem inspired the music for *Swan Lake*. To entertain his sister's young children, he wrote the music for *The Sleeping Beauty*. Even more famous is *The Nutcracker*, a ballet beloved around the world. While writing it, Tchaikovsky asked a friend in Paris to send him a new instrument called a celesta. It is the celesta that gives the special sound to "The Dance of the Sugar Plum Fairies."

In the summer of 1893, Tchaikovsky finished his Sixth Symphony, known as the *Pathetique*. He wrote to his nephew, "I certainly regard it as quite the best . . . of all my works. I love it as I never loved any one of my musical offspring before."

In November he had some stomach trouble. At the time, a cholera epidemic was raging in St. Petersburg, and it was well known that ordinary tap water was unsafe. Yet, to calm his stomach, Tchaikovsky drank it. Three days later he was dead.

"My ideal?" he said as a young man, "My ideal is to become a good composer." He succeeded, but the man who thrilled millions with his music once wrote, "I am not happy, not happy, not happy...happiness does not exist for me."

CHAPTER 9

"ONE DAY I SHALL BE THE PRINCESS"—ANNA PAVLOVA

On a wintry January night in 1890, eight-year-old Anna Pavlova excitedly hopped into a sleigh. Her mother had carefully saved up money for seats in the upper balcony of the Maryinsky Theater in St. Petersburg. Later Anna recalled this night:

> When we set out for the Maryinsky, the snow that had just fallen glistened in the reflection of the street lights, and our sleigh slid noiselessly over the frozen streets. Seated beside my mother, her arm around my waist, I was suffused with happiness.
>
> "You are going to see the country of the fairies," she said as we were rapidly drawn through the night toward the unknown, mysterious thing which was the theatre.
>
> The ballet was *The Sleeping Beauty* with Tchaikovsky's enchanting music. From the first measures of the orchestra I became very grave and began to tremble, troubled for the first time by the thrill of the beautiful.

This visit to the ballet was a turning point in Anna Pavlova's life. Her mother, amazed at Anna's strong reaction, asked if she would like to dance with the ballet troupe someday. "One day I shall be the Princess," Anna said, "and shall dance upon the stage of this theater." It was a promise that Anna would keep. Not only at the Maryinsky but on stages throughout the world, she would be the "Princess" of her art.

Born on January 31, 1881, in St. Petersburg, Anna was a delicate and weak baby. Her mother, a laundrywoman, feared she would not survive and took her to a church to be baptized on February 3. Since this was St. Anna's day in the Russian Orthodox calendar, the child received that name. During her childhood she suffered from various illnesses, including scarlet fever and diphtheria.

Anna and her mother lived by themselves in a little apartment. Anna described it later:

> We were very poor but nevertheless my mother always found the means to provide me with an unexpected treat on holidays. At Easter some toys were hidden in my huge Easter egg and at Christmas we always had our little fir tree decorated with gilded fruits and glittering in the light of candles.

After seeing the performance of *The Sleeping Beauty*, Anna pleaded with her mother to take her to the Imperial Ballet School for lessons. But the school did not accept children younger than ten. Soon after her tenth birthday, Anna applied. She was examined to see if she could meet the exacting standards of the school. The teachers watched her walk and run across the floor, also testing her in singing, reading, writing, and arithmetic. The competition was keen because the Imperial Ballet School provided a free education and it was a great honor to be in ballet in Russia.

Although ballet had developed in France and Italy in the seventeenth century, the classical dance tradition took root in Russia during the time of Catherine the Great. Russian dancers brought the ballet to its highest peak. Anna gave a possible explanation:

> We Russians dance because to us dancing is a true ideal, one perfect in itself. Possibly this is an outcome of the fact that Russia is the home of folk-dancing and that for centuries we have immortalized in action...those beautiful legends of folklore which other nations have confined to books.

Though the honor of being accepted at the famous school was great, so was the work and discipline. As Anna commented:

> To enter the School of the Imperial Ballet, is to enter a convent where frivolity is banned, and where merciless discipline reigns. Every morning at eight, the solemn tolling of a big bell would put an end to our sleep. We dressed under the stern eye of a governess, whose duty it was to see that all hands were kept perfectly clean, all nails in good trim, and all teeth carefully washed. When we were ready, we went to prayers which were sung by one of the older pupils in front of an icon under which a tiny flickering lamp was burning like a little red star. At nine, breakfast—tea, bread and butter—was served, and immediately afterwards the dancing lessons began.

For eight years Anna lived at the school, seeing her mother only on Sundays and holidays. As part of her training, she learned fencing, dancing, acting, playing the piano, and the skills of applying cosmetics and designing costumes. In the afternoons, students took the usual school subjects. All the girls wore a white apron over a blue serge dress that reached to their feet. White stockings and black pumps completed the uniform. Another part of the school taught boys, but the sexes were kept carefully segregated.

Two years after she arrived, Anna played a lotus bud in the school's annual performance for the czar's birthday. It was followed by a festive supper where the girls met the czar and his family. After one of these presentations, Alexander III kissed a girl who had given a particularly brilliant performance. "This was a sad day for me," wrote Anna. "I shed bitter tears of jealousy and stamped my feet. To console me, the Grand Duke Vladimir let me ride on his knee! But still my grief knew no bounds, as I said that the Emperor ought also have taken me in his arms and kissed me."

Anna's ballet teachers, the best in Russia, soon saw her special talents. Although she was not as strong and athletic as some dancers, she had a fluid grace and beautiful line of body that was unique. The school's greatest choreographer, or designer of dances, was Marius Petipa, who developed many of Tchaikovsky's ballets. He put Anna's talents on display, pairing her with Michael Fokine, a young dancer and a budding choreographer himself.

After her graduation performance in 1899, Pavlova joined the Imperial Ballet troupe. In her first performance at the Maryinsky, she showed her special stage presence. While pirouetting, Anna tripped over the prompter's box and fell with a thump to the floor. Unruffled, she rose gracefully, smiling and curtsying to the audience as if this was just part of the ballet.

By Pavlova's second season, she was dancing lead roles. Her performance of *Giselle* made her the toast of St. Petersburg. One critic wrote, "Her dancing is like the flying sound which comes from a harp." In 1906 she received the highest official title of *prima ballerina* and began dancing with Vaslav Nijinsky.

Nijinsky was the greatest male dancer of the time, and the only rival to Pavlova's star status. His great leaps electrified audiences, and he had as vivid a stage presence as Anna did. The competition between the two seemed to spur both of them to greater heights. Later, Nijinsky's wife wrote that Pavlova had once fainted with jealousy when he received more curtain calls than she had.

In 1906 Michael Fokine choreographed the first of a series of ballets for Pavlova. Called *Les Sylphides*, it was based on the music of the Polish composer Frederic Chopin. Fokine wrote:

> Pavlova flew across the entire stage during the mazurka [a Polish dance]. If one measured this flight in terms of inches, it actually would not be particularly high; many other dancers jump higher. But Pavlova's position in midair, her slim body— in short, her talent—consisted in her ability to create the impression not of jumping but of flying through the air. Pavlova had mastered the difference between jumping and soaring, which is something that cannot be taught.

Fokine also created what was to be Pavlova's most famous ballet piece—*The Dying Swan*. Fokine had been struck by the beauty of Camille Saint-Saens' composition, *The Swan*. When he suggested dance steps for it, Anna was enchanted. It was perfect for her talents. Through endless hours of practice, she perfected the movements of her whole body in a graceful longing for life and a fear of death. Anna made it her signature dance.

She made her first tour outside of Russia in 1908, going to Sweden, Denmark, Germany, and Austria. In Stockholm, the Swedish king sent a carriage to bring her to the palace. After her performance a crowd gathered at the balcony of her hotel and would not leave even after she threw down flowers. Her maid's comment about why they were so enthusiastic struck a chord in Anna: "Madam, you have made them happy by letting them forget for one hour the sadnesses of life."

The next year, between performances in Russia, Anna appeared in Paris. She came with Russia's greatest dancers under the sponsorship of Sergei Diaghilev. A true showman, Diaghilev was dedicated to bringing Russian culture to the world. He paired Pavlova with Nijinsky again, and their dancing caused a sensation. The Paris newspapers raved: "This one is a glory....A sacred flame burns in her....when she dances, the result is that undefinable thing, a masterpiece."

Diaghilev offered Pavlova the starring role in a new ballet called *The Firebird*, with music by Igor Stravinsky, a young Russian composer. Stravinsky's modern music was very different from traditional forms. Pavlova turned down the role. This led to a disagreement with Diaghilev, and she left his troupe for good.

The last time Pavlova danced in Russia was in 1914. Later that year, while she was on tour, World War I broke out in Europe. It led to the Russian Revolution of 1917, and brought a Communist government to power. Pavlova never returned to her homeland, but she was to take the ballet all over the world.

Pavlova gathered together her own dancers and toured the United States and Canada. She not only played in New York and San Francisco, but in many smaller cities where ballet had never been seen. She often danced in halls and clubs that did not have ideal facilities. In Montgomery, Alabama, she performed in a theater with a hole in the roof. It rained—during a performance of *Snowflakes*—and the dancers had to avoid puddles on the stage. "Never mind," said Pavlova, "these are the people who need us and it gives me more joy to dance for them than at the Metropolitan Opera House."

When Pavlova went to Cuba, she was upset when almost no one appeared for the performance. As it happened, a revolution

had broken out, and she and her troupe had to flee on a banana boat. She went on to South America. In Venezuela the dictator Juan Gomez wanted to see her dance *Coppelia*. But it was Sunday and the orchestra refused to rehearse. The dictator threatened to jail the musicians if they did not show up. In Mexico, Anna performed in the bullring so that more people could see her. Rain fell, and though she tried to continue, the mud made it impossible, causing a riot.

After the war, Pavlova bought a home in Great Britain, where she opened a school to train budding dancers. By all accounts she was a stern mistress, insisting on perfection through constant practice. Before one performance she discovered that the company had not rehearsed that day. She scolded them, "I am Anna Pavlova, you are my *corps de ballet*. I practice every day, while you do nothing." While the audience waited, stamping their feet impatiently, she led the group through ballet exercises before letting the curtain rise.

In 1922 Pavlova took her company to Asia. Although the audiences were unfamiliar with ballet, she was a huge success. A Japanese novelist described her performance in *The Dying Swan*: "As I gazed upon [her] arms and legs...the neck and wings of the swan seemed to emerge, accompanied by the wake and ripple of the lake; I even heard the soundless voice—I could not believe my senses. Pavlova became magnificent."

A dancer's career is usually short because of the physical demands of the art. Pavlova's incessant travels put a further strain on her. Yet she refused to retire. Before a performance in St. Louis, she hurt her left ankle but told newspaper reporters that her right one was injured. "You see," she told her troupe, "now they will watch the right ankle during the performance, and nothing will seem amiss." The discipline that she had learned at the Imperial School stayed with her. Moreover, she felt a strong bond with her audiences and a zeal to bring the ballet to as many as possible.

In the beginning of 1931, she was in ill health but still chose to fulfill a commitment to dance in the Netherlands. Arriving on January 17, she was rushed to a hospital, where the doctors said she had pleurisy. Anna insisted she would perform anyway. But her condition worsened. Five days later, it was clear death was near. Right after midnight she tried to cross herself. "Get my Swan costume ready," she whispered to her maid. A half hour later she was dead. The day was January 23—a week before her fiftieth birthday.

C H A P T E R 10

"A PROPHECY OF REVOLUTION"— VERA ZASULICH

Early in the morning of January 24, 1878, Vera Ivanovna Zasulich hurried through the cold, gloomy streets of St. Petersburg. She headed toward the office of the governor-general of the city— the hated Fyodor Trepov. There was no turning back now, Vera thought. She had to act. Within her fur muff she carried a revolver.

At the office about ten people had already gathered, hoping to persuade Trepov to grant their petitions. Military guards escorted Trepov into the office, and he began to move down the line of people. Vera later recalled:

> Now Trepov and his entourage were looking at me, their hands occupied by papers and things, and I decided to do it earlier than I had planned—to do it when Trepov stopped opposite my neighbor, before reaching me. And suddenly there was no neighbor ahead of me—I was first.... It's all the same; I will shoot when he stops next to the petitioner after me, I cried inwardly. The momentary alarm passed at once, as if it had never been.

When Trepov asked Vera what she wanted, she mumbled a few words. Suddenly the revolver was in her hand. She fired one shot, then another, and Trepov crumpled to the floor.

"Now they'll start beating me," Vera thought. She had rehearsed everything in her mind beforehand. But someone stopped the beating, shouting, "We must have an investigation." Vera saw to her surprise that she was the only calm person in the room.

Her hands were bound and she was turned over to two guards. One of them whispered in her ear, "Where did you learn how to shoot?"

"I learned! It's no big deal," Vera answered.

66

"You learned, but not enough," said the other guard. "It didn't hit right." Vera discovered at that moment that Trepov was only wounded. But her gunshots echoed all over Russia.

The future revolutionary was born in 1849, the youngest of three daughters of a gentry (landowner) family. When her father died, Vera was sent to live with a wealthy uncle in Bialkovo, a town in central European Russia. At the age of 11, Vera became very religious. She spent long hours praying before the icons on her uncle's estate. She prayed fervently to God and Christ for a good life. Young women of good family and limited education, like her, either married or took positions as governesses with wealthy families. Vera dreamed of doing something out of the ordinary:

> Even before I had revolutionary dreams, even before I was placed in boarding school, I made elaborate plans to escape becoming a governess. It would have been far easier, of course, had I been a boy: then I could have done almost anything....
>
> And then, the distant specter of revolution appeared, making me equal to a boy; I, too, could dream of "action," of "exploits," and of the "great struggle."

Russia was a divided society during the nineteenth and early twentieth centuries. The vast majority of Russians were peasants. Though they were no longer serfs, many still lived in primitive conditions. Yet most peasants revered the czar as a man designated by God to rule them.

But a strong current of social unrest stirred the Russian upper class. Like Tolstoy, they had been humiliated by Russia's defeat in the Crimean War. Many members of the gentry blamed Russia's backwardness on the autocratic rule of the czar. Russia had no constitution and no legislature; the czar was all-powerful. His censors had to approve all books and newspapers, and his secret police sent spies everywhere, watching for disloyalty of any kind. Talk of radical change—even revolution—was in the air.

Vera's life changed when she read a poem about the Decembrist Revolt of 1825. At boarding school, she attended lectures given by radicals who preached the heady ideas of revolution. She thrilled to the idea of reforming the country. Vera exchanged one religion, Christianity, for a new one: revolution.

After completing school at 17, Vera went to St. Petersburg

where she found work as a clerk. Like other young people of the 1860s, she looked for an outlet for her idealism. Vera volunteered to teach in a night school where workers learned to read and write.

Then she met Sergei Nechaev, the leader of a radical student group from the University of St. Petersburg. Nechaev was utterly devoted to the cause of revolution. He wrote that a true revolutionary was a "doomed man" who should have "no love, no friendship, no joy" outside the cause. In his view anything that helped the revolution was justified. Nechaev demanded absolute obedience from his followers; when he suspected someone of treachery, he ordered him killed.

Hearing that the police were about to arrest him, Nechaev fled the country. However, he continued to write his followers in St. Petersburg. The police intercepted his letters and rounded up everyone named in them. Vera was locked up in a St. Petersburg prison for two years and then exiled to the far north for two more years. Such punishment only toughened Vera and made her a more determined revolutionary.

After regaining her freedom in 1873, she went to live at Kharkov, where she enrolled in medical school. Here she joined another radical group, part of the Populist movement. The Populists' slogan was "Go to the People." Idealistically, they planned to live among the peasants and learn from them, while at the same time organizing them for revolution.

The movement was not very successful, for the cultural gap between the Populists and the peasants was too great. Raised with servants to do all the household chores, Vera was incapable even of making a bed. When her group opened a tea shop in a small village, it failed. Vera refused to make the traditional Easter pastry that peasants loved, and she couldn't make tea that any peasant wanted to drink. Furthermore, the Populists' talk of revolution made the peasants uneasy.

Three years later Vera returned to St. Petersburg. Her zeal had not dimmed; she worked for an underground printing press that produced revolutionary pamphlets. When she heard that Trepov, the governor-general of the city, had sentenced a radical student to be beaten with a birch rod, she was enraged. (The student had refused to remove his cap in Trepov's presence.) She hatched her plot to kill General Trepov.

Though she failed, the trial that followed riveted the attention of the country. Vera's defense lawyer turned her trial into an indictment of Trepov's brutal and corrupt administration. The jury listened with fascination to days of testimony about the cruelties of the police. Newspapers reported every word. Vera won the jury's sympathy when she testified that she hoped her act would "prove that no one who abused a human being that way could be sure of getting away with it....It's terrible to have to lift a hand against another person, but I felt it had to be done." When the jury came back with its verdict, the courtroom was hushed. Hearing the words "Not guilty," the spectators stomped their feet with approval.

The verdict in effect approved terrorism. Count Leo Tolstoy saw its meaning and worried about the future. He warned, "The Zasulich trial is no joke. This is like a prophecy of revolution." Five years later, in 1883, another group of revolutionaries did assassinate Czar Alexander II.

The czar had been outraged by the verdict in Zasulich's trial and ordered the police to take Vera into protective custody. However, friends hid her, and she eventually escaped to Switzerland.

Vera spent much of the next 25 years abroad, writing revolutionary pamphlets that were smuggled into Russia, and organizing groups to carry on the work. She met Georgi Plekhanov, another former Populist, who introduced her to the writings of Karl Marx. In 1881 Vera wrote to Marx to ask whether his ideas of revolution could apply to Russia.

Marx's name became a byword for revolution in the twentieth century. A German philosopher who spent years developing a theory of history, Marx saw that the industrial revolution had brought great wealth to a few people he called capitalists. These capitalists owned the factories where millions toiled for long hours at low wages. Marx predicted that the workers, or proletariat, would seize the factories and form communes that would run them for the good of all.

Marx felt that revolution would most likely occur in countries that were highly industrialized—not Russia. Still, Vera was undiscouraged; Russia had a small proletariat in the factories of St. Petersburg and Moscow. In 1883 she helped to found the first Russian Marxist party, the forerunner of the Russian Social-Democratic Workers' Party. In contrast to the Populists, the

Marxists placed their hopes in the urban working class rather than the peasants. Unlike Nechaev and his followers, the Marxists stressed organization, rather than terror, to attain their goals.

As the years went by, Vera spent time translating and writing in Switzerland and Britain. Because she had no family, she was often lonely and homesick. She wrote a friend that she spent her days in her tiny room with "incredible disorder." She wrote, brewed coffee and rolled a cigarette, then wrote some more. When she grew tired of writing, she read books. "So there's my life! I see no one, read no papers, and never think about myself."

However, she was not forgotten. Other exiled revolutionaries stopped by her apartment. In 1895, when she was 46, she met Vladimir Ulyanov. The world would know him as Lenin. Lenin had been only seven years old when Vera shot Trepov. His elder brother, a dedicated Populist, had been executed earlier for an attempted assassination of Alexander III. Like Vera, Lenin had rejected Populism and become a Marxist. He wrote his wife, "Wait till you meet Vera Ivanovna. There's a person as clear as crystal."

From their first meeting, Vera saw Lenin's fierce quality. She compared him to Plekhanov, who enjoyed discussing ideas far into the night. "Georgi is a greyhound," Zasulich said. "He shakes and shakes his adversary, then lets go. But you, you are a bulldog; you have a deadly bite." Lenin was pleased. "A bulldog, eh?" he said with a smile.

In 1900 Vera, Plekhanov, and Lenin started a newspaper called *Iskra*, or "The Spark." The name came from the promise of a Decembrist that "from this spark" of their revolt would come "the flame" of a revolution. Vera began to publish articles submitted by a writer who called himself "El Pero." Better known later as Leon Trotsky, he soon arrived and joined the group of Marxists around Vera. Trotsky was to become another of the major figures in the Russian Revolution.

In 1903 the members of the Social Democratic Party split. In some ways, Lenin was like Nechaev. He wanted the party membership to be limited to a small group of totally committed revolutionaries. Vera argued for a larger party that would welcome anyone who supported the movement's ideals. When Lenin won a vote on the issue, the party divided into two factions. Lenin called his group Bolsheviks, or the majority. Vera, Plekhanov, and their allies

were known as Mensheviks, or the minority. Lenin ruthlessly forced Vera and the other Mensheviks out of the inner circles of the party organization. From that point on, Vera would be on the sidelines as Russia took the final painful steps toward revolution.

In 1905 Russia lost a war with Japan. The humiliation was great, for this was the first time an Asian nation had defeated a European one. When the czar's troops fired on a group of demonstrators in front of the Winter Palace at St. Petersburg, a spontaneous revolution broke out. Workers formed groups of *soviets*, or councils, and the government seemed about to fall. But Czar Nicholas II appeased the strikers by promising new reforms, including an elected legislature, the Duma. Nicholas decreed a general amnesty for all political dissidents; after 27 years, Vera Zasulich was allowed to return home.

She lived quietly in a small apartment, corresponding with other Marxists who still hoped for a new day in Russia. An old friend from her Populist days came to visit, finding her sitting with a book "behind an incredibly messy table. On another table and on the windowsills there were plates with uneaten food, dirty glasses and teacups; in the corner soiled laundry of all kinds. Her bed was unmade. Yes, Vera Ivanovna remained herself to the end."

In 1914 World War I broke out and German armies invaded Russia. The Marxists and other revolutionaries discussed what their response should be. Should they support the Russian government or hope that the war would topple the czar's government? Lenin's Bolsheviks opposed Russia's involvement in the war. Vera was firm; Russia was her first love, and she urged others to support the war effort.

The war went very badly for Russia. It raised a massive army, but the soldiers were poorly supplied. Some men went to the front without any weapons except wooden clubs. At the 1914 Battle of Tannenburg alone, over 250,000 Russian soldiers died. The czar took personal command of the troops but was unable to turn the tide.

Finally, in 1917, the time was ripe for revolution. Exhausted by the war and frustrated by the scarcity of food at home, demonstrators appeared in the streets. This time the czar's troops refused to fire on them. Helpless, the czar abdicated. A new government was formed under the leadership of Alexander Kerensky, a lawyer who had been a schoolmate of Lenin's many years before. Unwisely, Kerensky refused to make peace with the Germans. More disturbances followed. Workers' soviets organized demonstrations to influence the Kerensky government.

For years Lenin had prepared for such an opportunity. Using the slogan "Land, Peace, Bread," his disciplined Bolshevik followers won the support of the soviets. In November 1917, they stormed the Winter Palace, overthrowing Kerensky's government. Lenin proclaimed a new soviet regime that eventually transformed Russia into the Soviet Union.

Vera Zasulich, who had worked so long for revolution, was now old and ill. She lived for only two years after the 1917 Revolution, without making any further public statements. She never saw what Lenin and his successors would do to Russia. But she might have recalled a letter that Karl Marx's collaborator, Friedrich Engels, wrote to her years earlier. Engels said, "People who imagined that they had made a revolution always saw next day that they did not know what they had been doing, and that the revolution which they made was nothing like the one they had wanted to make."

Vera could not have known how accurate a forecast that would prove to be.

"THE OCEAN OF CRUELTY"— SERGEI EISENSTEIN

On December 21, 1925, Sergei Eisenstein's new movie, *The Battleship Potemkin*, opened at the Bolshoi Theater in Moscow. As the audience took its seats in the theater, however, Eisenstein was still rushing to finish the movie.

For nearly three weeks, he had been working day and night to "cut" the film. In this process, a filmmaker splices together all the scenes that make up the finished movie. This was particularly time-consuming for Eisenstein, because he used many brief shots, lasting only a second or two, to heighten the excitement of his films.

He sent the first completed reel of film to the theater, and the movie started. Meanwhile Eisenstein remained at the laboratory frantically cutting the other reels. Throughout the next two hours, Eisenstein's assistant roared back and forth from the lab to the theater on a motorcycle. When the motorcycle broke down, he ran through the streets carrying the next reel. Eisenstein ran out of film glue and used spit to hold the very last bits of film together.

The effort was worth it. The audience greeted the movie with thunderous applause. Later, movie lovers throughout the world were equally enthusiastic. Today Eisenstein's masterpiece is still regarded as one of the very greatest movies ever made. Student filmmakers watch it over and over to gain ideas and inspiration from Russia's cinematic genius.

Sergei Eisenstein was born January 23, 1898, at Riga, in present-day Latvia. His father, of German-Jewish descent, was the chief architect of the city. Sergei's Russian mother, Julia, was elegant and pretty, but totally self-absorbed. She paid little attention to her young son.

The warmth in Sergei's life came from his nurse, an illiterate woman named Totya Pasha. From her, Sergei picked up superstitions that remained with him throughout his life. He feared Fridays and cats, and would not walk under ladders. Totya also took Sergei to the movies—early silent films that were only a few minutes long. A sensitive child, Sergei was terrified by a branding scene in one of these movies. He later said this experience was the source of "the ocean of cruelty" in his own films.

While attending school in Riga, Sergei met Maxim Strauch, who wanted to be an actor. The two would become lifelong friends. Sergei showed such talent for drawing that he won a scholarship to art school. But his father had other plans for his son. He sent Sergei to St. Petersburg in 1914 to enroll in engineering school.

Sergei spent his free time attending plays, operas, and vaudeville shows. He loved the theater and decided to make it his career. But in 1917 the Russian Revolution changed his life, as it did those of millions of others.

Though Lenin seized control of the government, opposition to his rule arose throughout Russia. From 1918 until 1920, Russia was consumed by civil war. Lenin assigned Leon Trotsky to organize the Red Army to defend the Bolshevik regime against its opponents, who were called "Whites." Eisenstein joined the Red Army and, because of his engineering training, was assigned to build defenses around the city—renamed Petersburg after the revolution. (It was later renamed Leningrad, but recently its residents have voted to restore the original name.)

After leaving the army in the late autumn of 1920, Eisenstein went to Moscow, the new capital of the country. In the aftermath of revolution and war, conditions were terrible. People were starving and Sergei had neither a ration book to get food nor a place to stay in the freezing weather. Wandering around the city, he ran into his old friend Max Strauch. Sergei moved in with him.

Eisenstein and Strauch searched for jobs in the Moscow theater and joined the Proletkult. This group aimed to create a new revolutionary theater to glorify the working people's struggle. Eisenstein's talent and originality swiftly won him the right to direct his own works. In 1924 he put on a play called *Gas Masks* in an actual gas factory to increase its reality.

Eisenstein became intrigued with the new possibilities of film. By now he had seen the movies of the American director D. W.

Griffith and the German film masters. Using them as models, he made a movie called *Strike*. Eisenstein wanted to make a story without stars, even without a regular story line. The hero was to be the working class itself. He filmed a series of scenes of workers preparing to strike. They resist all efforts to break their solidarity, but in the end the czar's feared cossack troops come in and massacre the workers. Eisenstein used unusual techniques for his effects. Juxtaposed with the scenes of the massacre is the slaughter of a cow. When *Strike* was released in 1925, a critic called it "the first revolutionary creation of our cinema."

Eisenstein's next project was a film to celebrate the twentieth anniversary of the 1905 revolution. He concentrated on one episode—the mutiny of the sailors on the battleship *Potemkin* in Odessa. Hearing of the revolution in St. Petersburg, the crew of the *Potemkin* rose up and killed their officers. They sailed the ship to the Odessa harbor and laid the body of a sailor in a tent near the pier. The people of the city came to pay respects, bringing food and flowers.

Then, in Eisenstein's movie, the cossacks appear at the top of the steps leading down to the harbor. The crowd wavers and then panics as the cossacks open fire. Many are killed in the terrible flight down the Odessa steps. The guns of the *Potemkin* fire salvos at the cossacks, but the ship is surrounded by a squadron of battleships. The men of the *Potemkin* use pennants to send the signal, "Don't fire, brothers." The *Potemkin* passes through the ring of steel and comes forward until the bow blacks out the screen.

Most of the people in the film were not actors at all. Eisenstein had his friend Max scour the streets of Odessa to find faces that matched the characters he had in mind. To film the famous scene of a baby carriage rolling down the Odessa steps, Eisenstein hired a circus acrobat to strap a camera to his waist and tumble down the steps with the camera running.

The worldwide success of *The Battleship Potemkin* made Eisenstein the most famous Russian filmmaker. However, he had jealous rivals who thought him too arrogant. Although he generously praised people he thought talented, he was scathing in criticizing those who did not measure up to his standards. People did not forget.

Soon he was planning an even greater project—a film called

October. It would depict the 1917 Revolution and the foundation of the new nation that in 1922 was renamed the Union of Soviet Socialist Republics (U.S.S.R.). Eager to help, the Soviet government allowed Eisenstein to use the Winter Palace for his film. The scene of the Bolshevik forces attacking the palace was so realistic that over 200 windows were broken.

However, Eisenstein ran into political problems. After Lenin died in 1924, Leon Trotsky and Joseph Stalin, secretary of the Communist Party (successor to the Bolsheviks), vied to take Lenin's place. As Eisenstein neared the end of filming, it was clear that Stalin would be the winner. Eisenstein was forced to cut all the scenes that showed Trotsky's role in the revolution. Almost one-third of the film was scrapped, and the movie was not as successful as Eisenstein had hoped.

On his next film Stalin himself ordered the ending changed. Eisenstein then decided to go abroad. From 1929 to 1932, he traveled through Europe, the United States, and Mexico. Everywhere he went, he was greeted with wild acclaim. He signed a contract with a Hollywood movie studio. Even there, however, he found that politics interfered with his art. When he made a movie attacking the capitalist system, the studio rejected it and canceled his contract.

On Eisenstein's return home, he found that Stalin had cracked down further on artistic freedom. All art now had to follow "socialist realism," which was little more than propaganda for the state. One of Eisenstein's enemies had been placed in charge of the national film industry, and he enjoyed making Eisenstein's life miserable. Nevertheless, Eisenstein started a new movie, trying to follow the demands of socialist realism, but a committee of Stalin's censors declared the film unacceptable. It was never shown publicly. Eisenstein appeared to be finished in the movie business.

Yet he was luckier than many other Soviet citizens in the 1930s. After the revolution, the lands that had belonged to the aristocracy were divided among the peasants. When small farms proved inefficient, Stalin set out to "collectivize" agriculture—to create huge state-owned farms. The plan resulted in chaos. Millions of Russian peasants were killed or died from starvation.

Stalin attributed his failures to "traitors." His secret police became as powerful and ruthless as any czar's. Old Bolsheviks, who had thought the revolution would bring freedom to Russia, now found themselves on trial for imaginary crimes. Stalin's firing squads mowed down anyone who presented the slightest threat to his rule—even those who had been Lenin's closest aides.

Fortunately for Eisenstein, Stalin enjoyed movies and saw that Eisenstein's talent could be useful. After Eisenstein made a public confession of his "errors," Stalin entrusted him with making a movie about Alexander Nevsky. It would glorify the Russian victory over the Teutonic Knights in the thirteenth century. The theme reflected Stalin's concerns about the growing power of Nazi Germany. Adolf Hitler, the German dictator, had rebuilt his country's military forces and seemed ready to make war.

Eisenstein began the filming with the high point of the movie—the battle on the ice between the valiant, dark-clad Russian army and the menacing Knights in ghostly white costumes. Because it was summertime, he used artificial snow, painted trees white, and covered a lake with "ice" floating on pontoons. The camera lens was covered with a filter to give the scenes a wintry look. The great composer Sergei Prokofiev wrote a musical score for the film.

Alexander Nevsky had its first performance in 1938. Soviet audiences loved it, and Stalin showed his approval by awarding Eisenstein the medal of the Order of Lenin. Within a year, however, the film was withdrawn. Stalin and Hitler had startled the world by signing a nonaggression pact—the Germans changed from Russian foes to partners. Eisenstein's anti-German film was now an embarrassment.

His career took another downward turn. Two films that he began were canceled. At this time Eisenstein was so depressed that he talked of suicide. Then he was given the post of artistic director of Mosfilm, the state film industry. Following the new "party line," he supervised a production of a German opera to show Stalin's "appreciation" for German culture.

Eisenstein's sense of purpose as an artist revived as he planned his most ambitious work—a three-film epic about Ivan the Terrible. This seemed a safe enough topic, for Ivan was one of Stalin's heroes. The official Soviet encyclopedia called Ivan "one of the great civilizers," and Stalin saw Ivan as the true founder of Russia. He once told Eisenstein that the only problem with Ivan was that he "didn't cut off enough heads."

Before filming could start, Germany suddenly invaded the Soviet Union on June 22, 1941. Hitler proved to be more treacherous than Stalin had thought. Mosfilm and its production facilities moved east to Kazakhstan. Eisenstein spent the next three years there, making part one of *Ivan the Terrible*. While the war raged, Eisenstein drove himself and his crew mercilessly. The combination of madness and greatness in Ivan the Terrible obsessed him. Eisenstein saw these same qualities within himself—and in Stalin.

By the fall of 1944, the tide of war had turned. Eisenstein returned to Moscow to make the final cut of his film. It opened in January 1945 to great acclaim. Eisenstein immediately began work on part two of the trilogy. This was the part that would contain the most dreadful of Ivan's cruelties. Eisenstein filmed one sequence in color, the first time he had used color film in his movies. In February 1946, on the day that he finished editing part two, Eisenstein went to a party to celebrate. While dancing, he suffered a heart attack.

For a while he hovered between life and death. On recovering, he learned for the first time that the Communist Party had condemned the second part of *Ivan the Terrible* as "unsuccessful" and "erroneous." Eisenstein publicly apologized, thanking the committee for this "stern and timely warning." His career as a filmmaker was finished.

In the remaining two years of his life, he continued to teach and write books on his art. Years before, a fortune-teller had told him he would die at the age of 50. The prediction came true. Despite Eisenstein's fall from official favor, Stalin gave him a grand state funeral in 1948.

CHAPTER 12

"A LIFE WORTHY OF OURSELVES"— ANDREI SAKHAROV AND ELENA BONNER

One day in December 1966, Andrei Sakharov found an envelope in his mailbox. It contained two thin sheets of paper. One described the plight of an artist who had been sent to a mental hospital. He had been declared insane for writing a model constitution to encourage a discussion of democracy in the Soviet Union.

The second sheet of paper announced a silent demonstration on behalf of the artist, at Pushkin Square in Moscow. Sakharov decided to go. When he arrived, he saw a few dozen other people gathered around the statue of Russia's famous poet. He described what happened next:

> At 6 o'clock, half of those present, myself included, removed our hats and stood in silence. (The other half, I later realized, were KGB [secret police].) After a minute or so, I walked over to the monument and read the inscription [on its base] aloud:
>
> I shall be loved, and the people will long remember
> that my lyre was tuned to goodness,
> that in this cruel age I celebrated freedom
> and asked for mercy for the fallen.

This act changed Sakharov's life. Already one of the country's most respected scientists, he stepped forth to protest the lack of freedom in the Soviet Union. Drawn into the struggle for human rights, he met and married another freedom activist, Elena Bonner. Together they took on the all-powerful Soviet state.

Andrei Sakharov was born in Moscow on May 21, 1921, the son of Ivan and Ekaterina Sakharov. They lived in a communal apartment house with four other families, all relatives of theirs. His father was a science teacher, and from a young age Andrei loved to do experiments. From his grandmother he acquired a love for Russian literature.

"I grew up," Andrei later wrote, "in an era marked by tragedy, cruelty, and terror." Before he reached his teens, Stalin's Great Terror had begun. The dictator ruthlessly sought to stamp out any opposition, real or imagined. Stalin's Terror devastated millions of Russian families, and the Sakharovs were not spared. Andrei's uncle and other relatives were among those who were arrested and sentenced to prison or exile.

Andrei showed great academic promise and graduated from high school at the top of his class. In the fall of 1938, he enrolled as a physics student in Moscow University. On June 22, 1941, in his third year, all the students were suddenly called into the auditorium and told that Nazi Germany had invaded the Soviet Union. Everyone was called on to contribute to the country's defense. Sakharov repaired radio equipment for the army in a university workshop and joined a volunteer air defense unit. As the German troops approached Moscow, Sakharov and the other students were moved to safety in Central Asia, where his studies continued.

Sakharov's professors recognized his brilliance. After the war he was invited to study with Igor Tamm, one of the Soviet Union's best physicists. Sakharov soon attracted the attention of the scientists in charge of the Soviet weapons program.

In the closing days of World War II, the United States had opened the nuclear age with the atomic bombings of Hiroshima and Nagasaki in Japan. Though the United States and the Soviet Union had been allies in World War II, Stalin wanted atomic weapons of his own. Relations between his regime and its wartime allies had cooled in the postwar period. When the U.S.S.R. seized control of eastern Europe, the United States moved to stop the spread of communism. The Cold War struggle between the United States and the Soviet Union had begun.

In 1948 Sakharov joined the Soviet atomic weapons program. He was soon working on an even more powerful nuclear weapon— the hydrogen bomb. He later wrote, "When I began working on this terrible weapon, I felt subjectively that I was working for peace, that my work would help foster a balance of power." Sakharov's

contribution was so important that he became known as the father of the Soviet hydrogen bomb.

In the 1950s Sakharov began to worry about the dangers of atomic fallout. Nuclear weapons tests released radioactive particles into the air. Radioactivity from this fallout began to show up in people's bodies. High rates of cancer resulted, and no one knew what other effects might appear. After Stalin died in 1953, Sakharov appealed to the new Soviet leader, Nikita Khrushchev, to end aboveground nuclear testing.

Khrushchev and his successors relaxed some of the harsher aspects of Stalin's rule. But the Communist Party remained the only political party, and the government still refused to allow freedom of speech. Sakharov's conscience gnawed at him, for he wanted his country to become truly free. Yet it was hard to speak out, for as a scientist, he enjoyed special privileges in Soviet society. People who did important work were rewarded with automobiles, country houses, and the right to shop in stores that sold food and products that ordinary people seldom saw.

After the protest in Pushkin Square, Sakharov learned that the KGB had filmed the demonstration. He received a warning that he could lose his job and privileges. Sakharov ignored the advice. He wrote an "underground manifesto" in which he discussed the problems of world hunger and pollution, and the need for the two superpowers to cooperate for the good of all. The manifesto was published in the United States in 1968, but in the Soviet Union it had to be copied and passed from person to person.

He began to speak out openly against the punishment of dissidents—those who criticized the Soviet system. He condemned anti-Semitism and the government's refusal to allow Soviet Jews to emigrate to Israel. The government stripped him of his scientific posts. If this was an attempt to silence him, it failed. He now appeared often in public demonstrations against the government's policies. During one of them, in 1970, he met Elena Bonner.

Elena Bonner was born in Moscow on February 15, 1923. She was the daughter of Gevork Alikhanov and Ruth Bonner, whose Jewish family came from Siberia. Both parents were ardent Communists, but when Elena was only 14, they were arrested in the Great Terror. "Never did I believe," Elena wrote later, "either as a child or as an adult—that my parents could have been enemies of the state. Their ideals...had been lofty models for me." Her father was executed and her mother was sent into exile until 1954. Elena went to live with her grandmother Bonner, taking her last name.

At the outbreak of World War II, Elena volunteered to work as a nurse serving in the front lines. A bomb hit her medical team, and Elena suffered a concussion and other wounds that left her almost blind in one eye. After her recovery, she returned to nursing on a medical train.

After the war, Bonner went to Leningrad (formerly St. Petersburg), to become a doctor. Medicine provided an outlet for her idealism. She practiced public health work and wrote for journals. Though she joined the Communist Party, she considered herself an independent thinker.

In 1968 Elena became disillusioned with the Party after the Soviet invasion of Czechoslovakia. Soviet tanks ousted a new Czech government, which had allowed its citizens to speak and write freely. The Soviets would not tolerate such freedoms.

Bonner now began to take an active role in the growing dissident movement. She helped publish underground newsletters to rally support for dissidents who were placed on trial. While visiting a friend who organized their legal defense, she met Sakharov. They married in 1972, and for the next two decades worked fearlessly for freedom in the Soviet Union, peace and justice in the world, and environmental concerns.

The KGB constantly harassed the Sakharovs. In 1973, Elena was summoned to the police station for questioning five times in 16 days. Although usually soft-spoken, she stared down the bureaucrats who tried to frighten her. Other dissidents were sent to mental hospitals, put on trial, or jailed. The Sakharovs escaped such treatment because of Andrei's fame and value as a scientist.

Yet the government did all it could to make their lives miserable. When Bonner's eyesight deteriorated, she applied for permission to visit a clinic in Italy. The government granted it only after months of delay.

While she was in Italy, her husband won the Nobel Peace Prize, the first Russian ever to receive this honor. When the Soviet government refused to let him accept it, she went in his place. On December 10, 1975, Elena stood before an audience in Oslo, Norway, to read his acceptance speech. She read:

Other civilizations, perhaps more successful ones, may exist an infinite number of times on the preceding and following pages of the Book of the Universe. Yet we should not minimize our sacred endeavors in this world, where, like faint glimmers in the dark, we have emerged for a moment from the nothingness of unconsciousness into material existence. We must make good the demands of reason and create a life worthy of ourselves and of the goals we only dimly perceive.

In these eloquent words, one can hear the scientist as well as the human rights activist.

After receiving the Nobel Peace Prize, Sakharov increased his criticism of Soviet society. He declared that the government had failed to fulfill the promises of Communist goals and ideas. State control of the economy resulted in shortages of goods such as food and clothing. Instead of the freedom revolutionaries like Vera Zasulich had hoped for, the Soviet system brought terror and repression.

In 1975 the United States, the Soviet Union, and other nations signed an agreement in Helsinki, Finland, guaranteeing basic human rights to their citizens. The Soviet dissidents saw this as a chance to further their cause. The Sakharovs established a watchdog group to monitor the Soviet Union's compliance with the Helsinki accords. Similar groups sprang up in other cities.

After the Sakharovs condemned the Soviet invasion of Afghanistan in 1979, the KGB exiled Andrei to the city of Gorky, 250 miles east of Moscow. No Western news reporters were there.

Elena, still free to travel, became his link to the outside world.

Life at Gorky was a round of humiliations. Each time Elena visited, her purse was searched. Andrei's car was vandalized, and KGB agents watched his every move. Elena announced that she and Sakharov wanted to emigrate to end their "nightmarish existence." The Soviet government refused permission, citing Andrei's secret scientific information. The Soviet press accused Elena of being a foreign spy who was an evil influence on her husband. After a secret trial, Elena too was sentenced to exile in Gorky.

Under the stress, Elena's health began to fail. She and Andrei went on a hunger strike to force the Soviets to let her go abroad for an operation. Finally she received her visa. She flew to Italy in December 1985 and then went on to the United States, where she had a reunion with her family, including her mother and her son by a previous marriage. President Ronald Reagan promised that he would "do everything possible" to free Sakharov.

Just before Christmas 1986, the couple received a surprise when workers installed a new telephone in their apartment in Gorky. The next day they received a phone call from the new Soviet premier Mikhail Gorbachev. He told them that they could return to Moscow to live and work.

Gorbachev, in power only a year, had promised a policy of *glasnost* or "openness." He soon proved he was serious by releasing more dissidents from jail. When Gorbachev permitted the election of a new People's Congress, Sakharov ran for office, and won. From his seat in the Congress, Sakharov demanded a multi-party system, which he believed was essential for democracy.

Still fighting for justice, Sakharov died in December 1989. His wife continued their work, living through the tumultuous changes that brought a new, peaceful revolution to the country. Gorbachev had released pent-up forces that he could not control. When hard-liners attempted to overthrow him in 1991, the plot was defeated by Boris Yeltsin, who soon replaced Gorbachev as leader.

Startling the world, Yeltsin dissolved the Communist Party and then allowed the Soviet Union to break up into several smaller nations. In 1992 the name Russia once more appeared on the map of the world. The Soviet Union had been undermined by people whose only weapons were words and ideas. Andrei Sakharov and Elena Bonner were among the courageous heroes who led the way.

G L O S S A R Y

Ataman: Leader of a band of cossacks.

Bolsheviks: Literally, "the majority." A group led by Vladimir Lenin that took control of the Social Democratic Party in 1903. The tightly knit, disciplined Bolsheviks helped Lenin seize control of the country in 1917.

Boyar: A Russian noble, before the time of Peter the Great.

Boyarina: A female boyar.

Bylini: Cossack ballads.

Choreographer: A designer of dances.

Cold War: The struggle between the United States and the Soviet Union that began after World War II. It was called a "cold" war because the two nations never took direct military action against each other. Instead, they used economic, political, and military aid to win support in other countries for democracy or communism.

Communist Party: The ruling party of the Soviet Union. It was the successor to Lenin's Bolshevik Party.

Corps de ballet: The supporting dancers of a ballet company, who perform as a group and do not have solo parts.

Cossacks: Independent frontiersmen who in later years became soldiers who served the czar; the word originally meant "adventurer."

Czar: Traditional title of the Russian ruler from the time of Ivan the Terrible; it is the Russian form of Caesar.

Czarina: The wife of the czar.

Decembrists: A group of officers and aristocrats who took part in the Decembrist Revolt of 1825. When the plot to overthrow Czar Nicholas I failed, the conspirators were hanged or exiled. However, their example inspired many later Russian revolutionaries.

Duma: An elected legislature that was formed in response to the revolution of 1905.

Gentry: The landowning class of pre-revolutionary Russia.

Glasnost: "Openness," the name for the policy of Soviet premier Mikhail Gorbachev that permitted public criticism of the regime.

Icons: Religious paintings that are found in the churches and homes of Orthodox Christians.

Marxists: Followers of the German philosopher Karl Marx, who believed that the working class would lead the revolution. Russian Marxists' views contrasted with those of the Populists.

Mensheviks: Literally, "the minority." The group that lost the battle for control of the Social Democratic Party to their rivals, the Bolsheviks.

Nakaz: "Instruction" issued by Catherine the Great as a plan to reform Russian society.

Old Believers: Members of the Russian Orthodox Church who refused to accept church reforms in the seventeenth century. Some still follow what they believe to be the true form of the religion.

Oprichnina: The secret police of Ivan the Terrible; its members were called oprichniki.

Patriarch: A head of the Eastern Orthodox Church.

Philosophes: Eighteenth-century French thinkers who believed that the world should be looked at through reason rather than religious faith.

Populists: A group of nineteenth-century Russian revolutionaries who believed that they could encourage revolution by going among the peasants, learning from them while at the same time organizing them for revolution.

Prima ballerina: The lead female dancer in a ballet troupe.

Proletariat: In the theories of Karl Marx, the working class.

Proletkult: A theater group formed in Moscow after the Revolution to create a new kind of art to glorify the workers' struggle.

Serf: A farm worker who was bound to the land he or she worked on and thus was part of the landowner's property.

Soviets: Workers' councils that took part in the revolutions of 1905 and 1917. Vladimir Lenin named his new revolutionary government after them, to show he was supported by the workers.

Streltsy: The czar's military guard, before the time of Peter the Great.

Terem: The women's quarters of the Russian court, before the time of Peter the Great.

Veche: The ruling council of the city of Novgorod in ancient times.

BIBLIOGRAPHY

Antonov-Ovseyenko, Anton, *The Time of Stalin: Portrait of a Tyranny*, New York: Harper & Row, 1980.

Bacharach, A.L., ed., *The Music Masters: The Victorian Age*, London: Cassell & Company, 1952.

Billington, James H., *The Icon and the Axe: An Interpretive History of Russian Culture*, New York: Vintage Books, 1970.

Bobrick, Benson, *East of the Sun: The Epic Conquest and Tragic History of Siberia*, New York: Poseidon Press, 1992.

Dukes, Paul, *A History of Russia*, 2nd edition, Durham, NC: Duke University Press, 1990.

Durant, Will and Ariel, *The Age of Louis XIV*, New York: Simon and Schuster, 1963.

Engel, Barbara A. and Rosenthal, Clifford N., eds. and trans., *Five Sisters: Women Against the Tsar*, New York: Knopf, 1975.

Fonteyn, Margot, ed., *Pavlova: Impressions*, London: Weidenfeld and Nicolson, 1984.

Harrison, Jane and Mirrlees, Hope, trans., *The Life of the Archpriest Avvakum by Himself*, London: Hogarth Press, 1924.

Hingley, Ronald, *A Concise History of Russia*, New York: Viking, 1972.

Howe, Sonia E., *Some Russian Heroes, Saints, and Sinners*, Philadelphia: J.B. Lippincott, 1917.

Kerensky, Oleg, *Anna Pavlova*, New York: E.P. Dutton, 1973.

Kirchner, Walthere, *Russian History*, 7th ed., New York: Harper Collins, 1991.

Lamb, Harold, *The March of Muscovy*, Garden City, NY: Doubleday, 1955.

Lazzarini, John and Roberta, *Pavlova: Repertoire of a Legend*, New York: Schirmer Books, 1980.

Lincoln, W. Bruce, *In War's Dark Shadow: The Russians Before the Great War*, New York: The Dial Press, 1983.

———. *The Romanovs: Autocrats of All the Russias*, New York: The Dial Press, 1981.

de Madariaga, Isabel, *Russia in the Age of Catherine the Great*, New Haven: Yale University Press, 1981.

Massie, Suzanne, *Land of the Firebird: The Beauty of Old Russia*, New York: Simon and Schuster, 1980.

Nicholson, Harold, *The Age of Reason*, London: Panther Books, 1968.

Pares, Bernard, *A History of Russia*, New York: Vintage Books, 1965.

Pipes, Richard, *Russia Under the Old Regime*, New York: Collier Books, 1992.

Riasanovsky, Nicholas V., *A History of Russia*, 4th ed., New York: Oxford University Press, 1984.

Sakharov, Andrei, *Memoirs*, New York: Vintage Books, 1992.

Salisbury, Harrison E., *Black Snow, White Snow: Russia's Revolutions 1905-1917*, Garden City, NY: Doubleday, 1977.

Sokolova, Lydia, *Dancing for Diaghilev*, ed. by Buckle, Richard, San Francisco: Mercury House, 1989.

Tolstoy, Leo, *War and Peace*, Givian, George, ed. and trans., New York: W.W. Norton & Company, 1966.

Troyat, Henri, *Ivan the Terrible*, New York: E.P. Dutton, 1984.

———. *Tolstoy*, New York: Dell, 1967.

Ulam, Adam B., *In the Name of the People: Prophets and Conspirators in Pre-Revolutionary Russia*, New York: Viking, 1977.

Vernadsky, George, *Kievan Russia*, New Haven: Yale University Press, 1948.

Volkov, Solomon, *Balanchine's Tchaikovsky*, New York: Anchor Books, 1985.

Wakeman, John, ed., *World Film Directors*, vol. 1, 1890–1945, New York: H.W. Wilson, 1987.

Wallace, Robert, and eds. of Time-Life Books, *Rise of Russia*, New York: Time-Life Books, 1967.

Weinstock, Herbert, *Tchaikovsky*, New York: Knopf, 1959.

Wolfe, Bertram, *Three Who Made a Revolution*, New York: Dell, 1964.

S O U R C E S

Introduction:
page 4: "Our whole land..." Dukes, Paul, A History of Russia, p. 7.
page 4: "The spirit of the Highest..." Howe, Sonia E., Some Russian Heroes, Saints, and Sinners, p. 40.
page 5: "The Greeks led us..." Billington, James H. The Icon and the Axe, pp. 6-7.

Chapter 1: Alexander Nevsky
page 6: "If thou canst resist..." Howe, op. cit., p. 79.
page 6: "God is not with Might..." Ibid., p. 80.
page 8: "There appeared amongst us..." Ibid., p. 72.
page 9: "Men could not hear..." Ibid., p. 75.
page 9: "Judge, O Lord..." Ibid., p. 82.
page 11: "My dear children..." Ibid., p. 89.

Chapter 2: Yermak
page 14: "He generally drank..." Dukes, op. cit., p. 44.
page 16: "a vast domain to Russia..." Troyat, Henri, Ivan the Terrible, p. 229.
page 17: "On the Volga..." Howe, op. cit., p. 209.

Chapter 3: Avvakum and Feodosia Morozova
page 20: "was given to..." Harrison, Jane, and Mirrlees, Hope, trans., The Life of Avvakum, p. 42.
page 21: "I am untutored..." Billington, op. cit., p. 126.
page 21: "I kept saying..." Ibid., p. 157.
page 22: "She kept law and order..." Howe, op. cit., p. 335.
page 24: "dancing bears..." Harrison and Mirrlees, op. cit., pp. 101-102.
page 24: "Run and jump..." Billington, op. cit., p. 157.

Chapter 4: Peter the Great
page 28: "to break the bonds..." Massie, Suzanne, Land of the Firebird, p. 91.
page 31: "Either change your character..." Durant, Will and Ariel, The Age of Louis XIV, p. 407.

Chapter 5: Catherine the Great
page 32: "The Grand Duke loved me..." Nicholson, Harold, The Age of Reason, p. 166.
page 34: "To tell the truth..." Ibid., p. 168.
page 35: "For eighteen years..." Ibid., p. 169.
page 36: "You philosophers are..." Ibid., p. 186.
page 38: "Enthroned in Russia..." Ibid., p. 188.

Chapter 6: Alexander Pushkin
page 39: "O you who return..." Massie, op. cit., p. 202.
page 41-42: "His hair cut..." Ibid., p. 206.

page 42: "O, but if my voice..." Lincoln, W. Bruce, The Romanovs, p. 494.

page 43: "Do you know how..." Massie, op. cit., p. 207.

page 44: "an encyclopedia..." Ibid., p. 207.

page 45: "You, like first love..." Riasanovsky, Nicholas V., A History of Russia, p. 357.

Chapter 7: Leo Tolstoy

page 46: "I am sure..." Troyat, Henri, Tolstoy, p. 119.

page 46: "It is good to be alive..." Ibid., p. 102.

page 48: "the most powerful impression..." Massie, op. cit., p. 310.

page 50: "If this game comes out..." Ibid., p. 311.

page 50: "Is it possible..." Pipes, Richard, Russia Under the Old Regime, p. 758.

page 50: "Denisov...unhooked his saber..." Gibian, George, trans., War and Peace, pp. 361-362,

page 51: "All this winter..." Massie, op. cit., p. 314.

page 52: "The kingdom of God..." Billington, op. cit., p. 298.

page 52: "Stop the machine..." Massie, op. cit., p. 324.

Chapter 8: Peter Tchaikovsky

page 55: "Oh, the music!..." Weinstock, Herbert, Tchaikovsky, p. 13.

page 56: "By nature I am a savage...." Bacharach, A.L., ed., The Music Masters, p. 340.

page 57: "The overture will be very loud..." Weinstock, op. cit., p. 224.

page 57: "I passionately love Russia..." Massie, op. cit, p. 342.

page 57: "The greater reason..." Bacharach, op. cit., p. 342.

page 58: "I certainly regard it..." Ibid., p. 346.

page 58: "My ideal?..." Ibid., p. 348.

page 58: "I am not happy..." Ibid., p. 345.

Chapter 9: Anna Pavlova

page 59: "When we set out..." Fonteyn, Margot, ed., Pavlova: Impressions, p. 17.

page 59: "One day I shall be..." Kerensky, Oleg, Anna Pavlova, p. 5.

page 60: "We were very poor..." Fonteyn, op. cit., p. 17.

page 60: "We Russians dance..." Kerensky, op. cit., p. 127.

page 60: "To enter the school..." Ibid., p. 7

page 62: "This was a sad day..." Fonteyn, op. cit., p. 21.

page 62: "Her dancing..." Kerensky, op. cit., p. 17.

page 63: "Pavlova flew..." Lazzarini, John and Roberta, Pavlova, p. 22.

page 63: "Madam, you have made them happy..." Ibid., p. 31.

page 63: "This one is a glory..." Ibid., p. 34.

page 64: "Never mind..." Ibid., p. 53.

page 64: "I am Anna Pavlova..." Kerensky, op. cit., p. 77.

page 65: "As I gazed..." Fonteyn, op. cit., p. 109.

page 65: "You see..." Kerensky, op. cit., p. 123.

page 65: "Get my Swan costume ready," Ibid., p. 150.

Chapter 10: Vera Zasulich

page 66: "Now Trepov and his entourage..." Engel, Barbara A. and Rosenthal, Clifford N., Five Sisters, p. 81.

page 68: "Even before I had..." Ibid., p. 69.

page 70: "prove that no one..." Ibid., p. 78.

page 70: "The Zasulich trial..." Lincoln, W. Bruce, In War's Dark Shadow, p. 160.

page 71: "So there's my life!" Engel and Rosenthal, op. cit., p. 93.

page 71: "Wait till you meet Vera..." Wolfe, Bertram, Three Who Made a Revolution, p. 137.

page 71: "Georgi is a greyhound..." Ibid., p. 107.

page 72: "behind an incredibly messy..." Ulam, Adam B., In the Name of the People, p. 274.

page 73: "People who imagined..." Wolfe, op. cit., p. 116.

Chapter 11: Sergei Eisenstein

page 76: "the ocean of cruelty," Wakeman, John, ed., World Film Directors, p. 291.

page 79: "didn't cut off enough heads," Antonov-Ovseyenko, Anton, The Time of Stalin, p. 212.

page 80: "stern and timely warning," Wakeman, op. cit., p. 304.

Chapter 12: Andrei Sakharov and Elena Bonner

page 81: "At 6 o'clock..." Sakharov, Andrei, Memoirs, p. 273.

page 82: "I grew up..." Ibid., p. 20.

page 82: "When I began working..." Ibid., p. 24.

page 84: "Never did I believe..." Current Biography Yearbook 1987, p. 60.

page 86: "Other civilizations..." Sakharov, op. cit., p. xiii.

INDEX

28, 32, 37, 41, 46, 48, 49, 52, 56, 70, 75, 76, 81, 82
Nakaz, 36
Narva, Battle of, 30
Nechaev, Sergei, 69, 71
Neva River, 6, 8, 30
Nevsky, Alexander, 6-11, 31, 79
Nicholas I, Czar, 43
Nicholas II, Czar, 72
Nicon, 20
Nijinsky, Vaslav, 62, 63
Novgorod, 6, 8, 10, 11, 14
Nutcracker, The, 58
Ob River, 17
Odessa, 77
Old Believers, 21, 22, 23, 24
Oprichnina, 14
Orlov, Gregory, 35
Pavlova, Anna, 59-65
Peipus, Lake, 9
Perm, 13
Peter I ("The Great"), 25-31, 37, 38, 41, 45, 48
Peter III, 32, 34, 35
Petipa, Marius, 62
Plekhanov, Georgi, 70, 71
Poland, 37
Poltava, Battle of, 30
Polvetsians, 8
Populists, 69, 70, 72
Potemkin, Gregory, 37-38
Prokofiev, Sergei, 79
Prussia, 37
Pugachev, Emelian, 36-37
Pugachev Rebellion, 36-37, 44
Pushkin, Alexander, 39-45, 51, 81
Reagan, Ronald, 87
Riga, 75, 76
Roman Catholicism, 4, 9
Rubinstein, Anton, 55, 56
Rubinstein, Nicholas, 56
Rurik, 4, 5
Rus, 4, 5
Russian Orthodox Church, 11, 18, 20-24, 29, 51-52, 59

Russian Revolution, 64, 73, 76
Russian Social-Democratic Workers' Party, 70, 71
St. Petersburg, 30-31, 38, 39, 41, 43, 44, 45, 48, 55, 58, 59, 62, 66, 68, 69, 70, 72, 76
Sakharov, Andrei, 81-87
Sebastopol, 38, 48
Serfs, 28, 49, 68
Siberia, 5, 15, 16, 17, 21, 24, 30, 36, 43
Soviet Union, 5, 73, 80, 81, 82, 84, 85, 86, 87
Soviets, 72, 73
Stalin, Joseph, 78, 79, 80, 82, 84
Strauch, Maxim, 76
Stravinsky, Igor, 63-64
streltsy, 28, 29
Stroganov family, 15
Suzdal, 9
Swan Lake, 58
Sweden, 6, 8, 9, 30, 63
Tartars, 8, 15, 16, 17
Tchaikovsky, Peter, 53-58, 59, 62
Terem, 22, 29
Teutonic Knights, 9, 10, 79
Tolstoy, Leo, 46-52, 68, 70
Tolstoy, Nicholas, 46, 48
Tolstoy, Sophia, 49, 51, 52
Trepov, Fyodor, 66, 68, 69, 70
Trotsky, Leon, 71, 76, 78
Turkish Empire, 37
Ulyanov, Vladimir, *See* Lenin.
Union of Soviet Socialist Republics, (U.S.S.R.) *See* Soviet Union.
Ural Mountains, 15
Vladimir, Grand Duke 4, 5
Vladimir (city), 9, 11, 13
Volga River, 13, 18, 37
Voltaire, 36
War and Peace, 50
Yasnaya Polyana, 46, 48, 49, 52
Yeltsin, Boris, 87
Yermak, 12-17
Zasulich, Vera, 66-73, 86